THE PRENTICE HALL GUIDE TO

EVALUATING ONLINE RESOURCES
WITH
RESEARCH NAVIGATOR

ENGLISH
2004

Melissa Payton
with contributions by Suzanne Drapeau

PEARSON

Prentice
Hall

UPPER SADDLE RIVER, NJ 07458

©2004 by PEARSON EDUCATION, INC.
Upper Saddle River, New Jersey 07458

ISBN 0-13-184085-1

Printed in the United States of America

Note: Research Navigator™ is continually expanded and updated. The screen shots included in this documentation may not reflect the latest updates. Refer to <http://www.researchnavigator.com/phguide/> to download the most recent documentation in either Microsoft® Word format or Adobe Acrobat® format.

Contents

Chapter 1

An Overview of Sources

What Are Sources?

When instructors speak of sources, they're usually referring to "outside" sources--materials outside your own knowledge or thinking that contain someone else's ideas. Sources provide information; they let you learn something you did not know before. Examples of legitimate sources include credible information from the Internet, library collections, and the spoken words of experts. They can be in the form of books, newspaper articles, interviews, television and radio programs, websites, maps, online databases, magazines, computer and video images, audiotapes, and academic journals. Sources add authority to what you write and nearly all college research assignments require their use.

Using sources well is the hallmark of sound nonfiction writing. Most research writing involves a combination of print and online sources. Although this guide will focus on online resources, the advice on evaluating sources--determining whether a website offers credible information that meets the standards of academic research--almost always applies to other sources as well.

Later chapters will help you use sources effectively in your writing. Chapter 2 will help you find online sources, use databases and search engines, and evaluate such sources for credibility. While the Internet is a nearly bottomless well of useful and enlightening information, it is also host to websites created by bigots, conspiracy theorists, and extremists--not to mention those who are well-intentioned but misinformed. Chapter 2 will help you sort the academically nutritious wheat from the Internet junk-food chaff.

Chapter 3 will help you avoid plagiarism, a cardinal sin. It will also acquaint you with paraphrasing and summarizing, and how to cite and document sources. Chapter 4 will introduce you to Research Navigator, a new online academic research service, and Chapters 5, 6, and 7 will show you how to use the service's three major databases. Chapter 8 will help you to use Research Navigator in a specific academic discipline.

Primary and Secondary Sources

Primary sources are firsthand evidence, based on your own or someone else's original work or direct observation. They can be documents, records, letters, diaries, novels, poems, short stories, autobiographies, interviews, and journals. This original quality adds to a source's reliability and impact on the reader.

Here is playwright Endesha Ida Mae Holland in her memoir, "From the Mississippi Delta" (1997):

> I was born into the double shotgun house at 114 East Gibb Street. Mama rented both sides of the clapboard house, which stood on raised posts. A confused patch of petunias hugged the ground at the end of the front porch. Inside, the crudely painted walls were peeling and patched with newspaper. The ceiling was so low that I could read "Little Lulu" on the funny pages pasted there. (pp. 19-20)

Holland goes on to describe the cracks in the linoleum floor that offered a view of the earth under the house and the patched roof that let in daylight and rain. Her brief account does more than describe a house: it tells us, indirectly but powerfully, about the poverty she was born into.

Secondary sources report, describe, comment on, or analyze the experiences or work of others. In college, most textbooks are secondary sources. As a piece of evidence, a secondary source is at least once removed from the primary source. It reports on the original work, the direct observation, or the firsthand experience. But it can have great value and impact as a source if the reporter or writer is reliable, either as a result of special experience (a journalist who spent years observing and reporting on the civil rights movement) or special training (a tooth-decay expert with a dental degree).

Newspapers are typical secondary sources. In a three-part series the *New York Times* published in January, 2003, reporters who examined the safety record of an Alabama-based pipe-making company concluded that it was "one of the most dangerous businesses in America." They based their conclusion on primary sources: company and government records and interviews with current and former employees, including plant managers, safety directors, and environmental engineers.

Here is a quote from the story:

> "The people, they're nothing," said Robert S. Rester, a former McWane plant manager who spoke at length about his 24 years with the company. "They're just numbers. You move them in and out. I mean, if they don't do the job, you fire them. If they get hurt, complain about safety, you put a bull's-eye on them." (Barstow & Bergman, Jan. 9, 2003, p. A1)

2

The *Times,* and most newspapers and magazines, are generally reliable secondary sources--although even highly-regarded publications make errors under the pressure of deadlines or competition. That's why sound research requires more than one source to back up a disputable claim.

Types of Sources

Print Sources

Newspapers, magazines, academic journals, documents, reference works, and personal papers are all print sources, although more and more of them exist in an online form as well.

For college research, the main tool for locating print sources that are not online is still the library. Many times you'll need to use electronic resources, especially the library catalog, to locate the print materials that you need to pull from the library's shelves. One major advantage of libraries: they come equipped with librarians. Reference-desk staffers can help you home in on the topic you need to research, come up with a research strategy, and determine the best tools to use in your research. The "Using Your Library" section of Research Navigator can also help you use a library's vast resources more efficiently.

Online and Database Sources

The Internet offers unlimited opportunities for research. Many print sources--newspapers, magazines, reference works, academic journals--are available online as well. One advantage of accessing print sources online, of course, is that you have millions of pages originating from across the globe at your fingertips. Another is that you can download and print a copy of an article for your files. Finally, many online-print sources are *searchable*: you can type a keyword into an archive or database to pull up the page you need. (Databases collect and organize content online so that users can find particular information. When did the "The Wizard of Oz" debut, and how many Oscars did it win? The Internet Movie Database, www.imdb.com, will tell you. Searching online databases is a skill of its own that will be covered in the next chapter.)

Online content that is *not* print-based is even more varied. The most useful sites for research usually are informational and have URL addresses that end in **.edu** or **.gov**. "Edu" websites are sponsored by educational institutions, and they may include research results, reference works, subject indexes, and databases useful in many disciplines. "Gov" sites, sponsored by government agencies, offer a trove of primary sources: census information, federal codes and regulations, licensing records, property data, and health statistics. Sites that end in **.org** are sponsored by a nonprofit organization, such as Planned Parenthood, the National Rifle Association, or Mothers Against Drunk Driving. Some "org" sites offer reliable, usable information--but remember that they are usually sponsored by a group or individual that seeks to influence public opinion.

Although most commercial sites (those with **.com** URLs) exist to sell merchandise, some do offer information useful to students and researchers at low or no cost. News sites are an example (www.nytimes.com, www.newsweek.com, www.washingtonpost.com). Most offer free access to at least the previous week's content. Unfortunately, more and more publications are charging for access to their archives--which contain the information most useful for research. Many college departments, however, buy a subscription to fee-charging online publications like the *Wall Street Journal* or news databases like LexisNexus. You will need to get a sign-on and password from your instructor or department office. (The online Research Navigator, www.researchnavigator.com, free with the purchase of any Prentice Hall college textbook, allows one-year access to the *New York Times*, along with searchable databases of academic and general interest publications and World Wide Web sites.)

Chapter 2

How to Find and Evaluate Online Sources

Finding Online Sources

Yes, there is a wealth of information on the Internet. In fact no one knows how many World Wide Web pages exist, because new ones are being created constantly--they number in the millions, certainly, and some say billions. But how do you find the information you need? And how do you make sure it is credible? Anyone with a few technical skills and access to a computer can publish on the Internet. Some sites offer information from experts; many sites are run by amateurs. Some sites are updated frequently; others, not at all.

To search the Web efficiently, it helps to be familiar with several different strategies and use the one that works best for your research topic. The two main vehicles for accessing information through the Internet are **subject directories** and **search engines,** which will be discussed in more detail in this chapter. If you try out several examples of both types, you will quickly find the search method you favor. Also, search engines and subject directories are not uniform in the techniques users must employ to narrow or broaden a search. So if you are comfortable with several methods of searching--using Boolean operators, truncation (or wild cards), and implied operators, also explained in this chapter-- you will be able to switch more easily from one search engine or subject directory to another.

Strategies for Searching the Web

Tailor your search to the scope of the information you are seeking. To do this, you will need to understand **search engines, subject directories**, and **specialized databases**. A subject directory will take you through a sequence of Internet subjects. You might start with "history," move to "military history," then to "Civil War history," "Civil War battles," and arrive finally at the Battle of Gettysburg, your goal. Internet search engines locate specific Internet sites devoted to your topic (such as Military History Online's "Battle of Gettysburg" site). They often feature both subject directories and keyword searches.

Specialized databases, which usually search a targeted topic or aspect of a topic, are sometimes hard to find with search engines, but there are websites that specialize in collecting links to them. All three of these types of searching tools are explained in greater detail later in this chapter.

The two most popular organizers of Web content are probably Yahoo! (www.yahoo.com) and Google (www.google.com). Google is known mainly for its search engine, admired by many for the way it produces highly relevant results. Google does offer other services (discussion forums, a subject directory, and news sources) and is regularly adding new ones. Yahoo!, which is older, is known more as a Web **portal**, or a site that offers a range of resources and services, including e-mail, on-line shopping, games, and chat forums. As an information resource, Yahoo! was once identified with its subject directory, in contrast to Google's search engine. But in recent years, Yahoo! has added a search engine. In 2002, Yahoo!'s search engine--and others--began using Google's database in response to Google's popularity, as well as to criticism that Yahoo! search results could be influenced by advertisers who paid for inclusion in its database. Both Google and Yahoo! now accept commercial listings, but they are identified as "sponsored links" or "sponsored matches" and grouped separately, usually at the top of the first results page. Use caution when considering using any information from a site seeking to sell a product (see "Evaluating Online Sources," later in this chapter).

Subject Directories

For general, research-oriented queries, for browsing, and to view sites recommended by experts, use a subject directory. There are two basic types: academic and professional directories, which are most useful to researchers, and commercial portals that cater to the general public.

Here are some commercial portals:

- **About.com**   www.about.com
- **Go.network**   www.go.com
- **Lycos**   www.lycos.com
- **Yahoo!**   www.yahoo.com

For example, in early 2003, Yahoo!'s homepage featured 14 major categories as links to further information. Clicking on "Health" would take you to another page, with dozens more subcategories. Clicking on the subcategory "Teen Health" resulted in links to 60 websites on the subject. They ranged from a government site aimed at helping girls become "fit for life" to a men's magazine site that emphasized selling products as much as offering advice. Yahoo! and other commercial sites do not evaluate user-submitted content when adding Web pages to a database; they leave the evaluation up to the user.

Academic directories, on the other hand, are often annotated by experts and are usually the result of much thought and care. To get started on finding such directories, try the University of Albany list of Internet Subject Directories (http://library.albany.edu/internet/subject.html). Other suggestions:

- **The Librarians' Index to the Internet** (www.lii.org). Sometimes called "the thinking person's Yahoo!."
- **The WWW Virtual Library** (www.vlib.org). One of the oldest and most respected subject directories on the Web. Many of the individual subject collections are maintained at universities.
- **INFOMINE** (infomine.ucr.edu). Compiled by the University of California at Riverside.

Search Engines

For targeted and complex queries, use a search engine. A search engine does not search the entire Internet; it searches **databases,** or collections of logically-related information, that are developed by the company hosting the search engine. That's why different search engines will produce different results. There are at least two ways for a page to be recorded in the search engine's database: the page's publisher can register it with the engine, or the search engine can use software called "spiders" to search the Internet and gather information that is then recorded in the engine's database.

Search engines may offer both subject directories and keyword searches. With most search engines, you enter your search terms and click on a "go" button or hit your return key. Then the engine generates a page with links to resources containing all or some of your terms. The resources are usually ranked by term: that is, one will rank higher if your search term appears many times, near the beginning of the document, in the title, and so forth.

A fairly recent development is a "second-generation" search engine, such as Google, which ranks Web pages according to the number of pages that link to them. This strategy adds an element of human judgment---in essence, it ranks a site by how popular it is--to computer technology. Many users start with Google, even for general queries, because it does such an excellent job of finding relevant documents.

Some popular search engines are:

- **AltaVista**   altavista.digital.com/
- **Excite**   www.excite.com
- **Google**   www.google.com/
- **Hotbot**   www.hotbot.com
- **Webcrawler**   www.webcrawler.com

Your choice of keywords to launch the search is just as important as your choice of search engine. Use the words you would like to find in the title, description, or text of an Internet site. Searching for a common or general word, such as "Clinton," will provide a massive search of every document that contains this term. (The lowercase **clinton** will find both upper- and lower-case instances of the term.) In fact, **clinton** generated 6.9 million results from Google, ranging from Hillary Clinton's official Senate Web page, to a biography of President Clinton, to a Clinton County, Mich., government site--all on the first results page. You'll get more usable results by narrowing your query. Do you want a biography of President Clinton? Clinton's stand on a particular issue? A chronology of Clinton's impeachment trial? Using more than one keyword will narrow your results and make them more relevant to your needs; even with thousands of results, most search engines will put the most relevant pages at the top of the results list.

It's also possible to conduct too narrow a search. If you combine keywords for something like "Ulysses S. Grant's military strategy at Gettysburg," you may produce few or no results. Try dropping one or more keywords until you get a usable list of links.

A **metasearch engine**, instead of creating its own database of information, searches the databases of several search engines. For example, when you enter a query at the Mamma.com website, the engine simultaneously queries about ten of the major search engines, such as Yahoo!, Webcrawler, and Magellan. It then provides you with a short, relevant list of results. **President Clinton impeachment** generated 62 results from Mamma.com, from search engines Teoma, Ask Jeeves, MSN.com, and others. Results included primary sources such as government documents and secondary sources such as press coverage--a mixture that might be useful in writing a college paper.

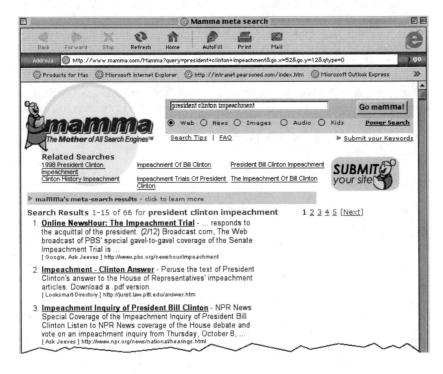

Ixquick is particularly helpful if your topic is obscure or if you want to retrieve results from several search engines without generating an enormous list. Ixquick returns only the top ten relevancy-ranked results from the source search services.

Some popular metasearch engines:

- **Ixquick**   www.ixquick.com
- **ProFusion**   www.profusion.com
- **Dogpile**   www.dogpile.com
- **Mamma.com**   www.mamma.com
- **Metacrawler.com** www.metacrawler.com

Using Boolean Terms and Other Search Limiters

When you use a search engine, you increase your chances of getting good results by formulating a precise query. Sometimes one word (or keyword) is sufficient, if it is distinctive enough.

Many times you can click on an advanced search option that will bring up a template to prompt you through the process. But sometimes it is helpful to know Boolean logic in order to narrow your search for manageable results.

Boolean logic comes from the ideas of British mathematician George Boole (1815-1864). From his writings come the Boolean operators: AND, OR, and NOT, used to link words and phrases for more precise queries for search engines and directories.

Increasingly, search engines are simplifying their search protocols by making "and" the default logic. If you type **president clinton impeachment** in most search engines, you will get results for the equivalent of **president** AND **clinton** AND **impeachment**.

Be sure to capitalize Boolean operators; some, but not all, search engines, will assume lowercase "and" or "or" to be part of a phrase and consider them "stop" words to be ignored. (Stop words are prepositions, articles, conjunctions, and other common words like **I, an, the, for**.) Most sites offer a link to a page that explains their defaults and other search protocols. From Google's homepage, for example, click on "Advanced Search" and then "Advanced Search Tips" to find this page:

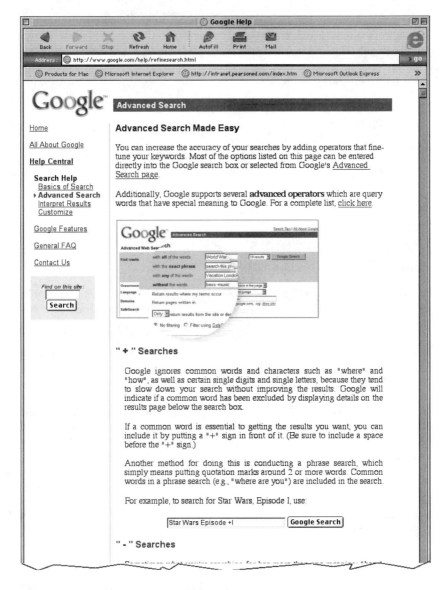

Boolean AND, OR, and NOT

The Boolean AND narrows your search by retrieving only documents that contain every one of the keywords you enter. The more terms you enter, the narrower your search becomes. Examples:

- gene AND therapy
- gene AND therapy AND risks

An Altavista search of **gene AND therapy** turned up more than 339,000 results; **gene AND therapy AND risks** generated 48,000.

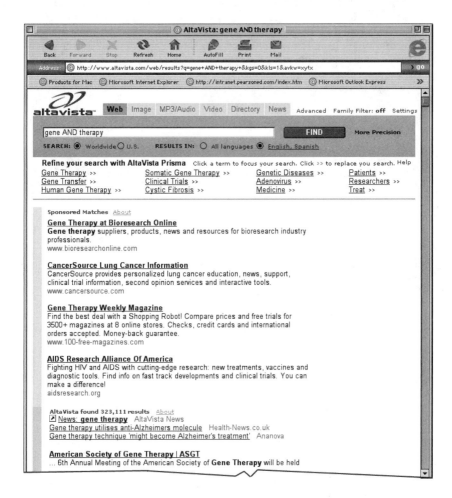

The Boolean OR expands your search by returning documents in which either or both keywords appear. Since the OR operator is usually used for keywords that are similar or synonymous, the more keywords you enter, the more documents you will retrieve. If you do a Google search of two keywords using OR and AND, you will see how OR broadens your search while AND narrows it:

- sea lions OR walruses (192,000 results)
- sea lions AND walruses (6,250 results)

The Boolean NOT or AND NOT limits your search by returning documents with only your first keyword but not the second, even if the first word appears in that document, too. For example, if you type in **seals** as a keyword, you'll get many results about Easter Seals. But if you wanted information on the animal, you could type:

- seals NOT Easter
- seals AND NOT Easter

11

Many search engines convert formal Boolean operators into more user-friendly template terminology when you enter their advanced search pages. The Google advanced search template gives you these options:

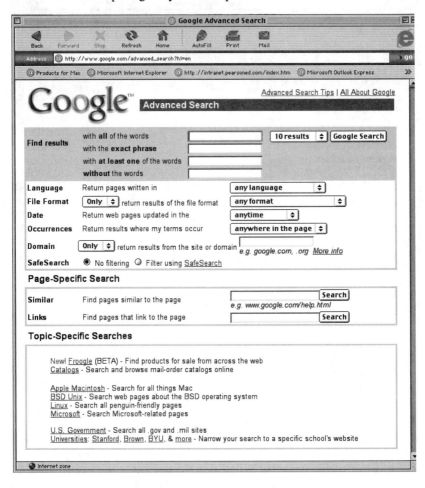

In the template above, "all the words" is equivalent to the Boolean AND; "at least one of the words," the Boolean OR; and "without the words," the Boolean NOT. "Exact phrase" means that if you type in **President Clinton,** you will get pages where **Clinton** is always preceded by **President**; if you use the "all the words" option and type **President Clinton**, you'll get pages with **President** and **Clinton,** but not necessarily together as a phrase.

Implied and Other Non-Boolean Limiters

While full Boolean operators are accepted in the advanced search option of some search engines, "implied" Boolean operators--or what some call "search engine math"--are accepted in the basic search options of an increasing number of search engines.

Implied Boolean operators use the plus (+) symbol for AND:

- gene +therapy +risks

The implied Boolean operator for NOT is a minus (-) symbol. Typing a (+) or (-) sign in front of a word will force the inclusion or exclusion of that word in the search statement.

- pinnipeds -walruses
- Star Wars Episode +I

Search engines have different rules about spacing before and after plus or minus signs. Google specifies a space before the symbol and no space after.

The "plus" technique is helpful when a key part of your search term is normally a stop word that a search engine would ignore. For example, typing **Star Wars Episode I** into Google will return results about all Star Wars episodes because Google will eliminate the "I" as a common word. Adding "+I" will return results only about Episode I.

Implied Boolean operators have no symbol for OR. A few search engines default to OR when two terms are searched (**war battle**), but most default to AND.

Quotation Marks

In most search engines, you can use quotation marks around two or more words to make them one unit (although proper names usually do not need quotation marks).

- "gene therapy risks"
- "SUV gas mileage"

Other Limiters

Proximity, or positional, operators--ADJ, for adjacent, or NEAR--are not really part of Boolean logic, but they serve a similar function in formulating search statements. Not all search engines accept proximity operators, but a few accept NEAR in their advanced search option. The NEAR operator allows you to search for terms situated within a specified distance of each other in any order. The closer they are, the higher the document appears in the results list. Using NEAR, when possible, in place of the Boolean AND usually returns more relevant results.

- sea lions NEAR pinnipeds
- Cheney NEAR Bush

With some search engines, you can truncate the word: use its root, followed by an asterisk, to retrieve variants of the word. For example, if you can't remember whether the organization is called Feminine Majority or Feminist Majority, you can enter **femini*** to find the site you want. This is also referred to as using a wild card or "stemming." Yahoo! supports wild card searches, but Google does not; if you don't get the results you want with one form of the word in Google, try the other (**walrus OR walruses**).

Another useful technique with some search engines is **field limiting,** which limits searches to a specified part of a page: title, URL, link, host, domain, image, or text, for example. Type in the field followed by a colon. If you wanted to make sure "multiple sclerosis" was in the title of a page in order to call up only sites devoted to the topic, you'd search for **title: multiple sclerosis**. Google uses "allintitle" for a title search, so a search for **allintitle: multiple sclerosis** would yield these results:

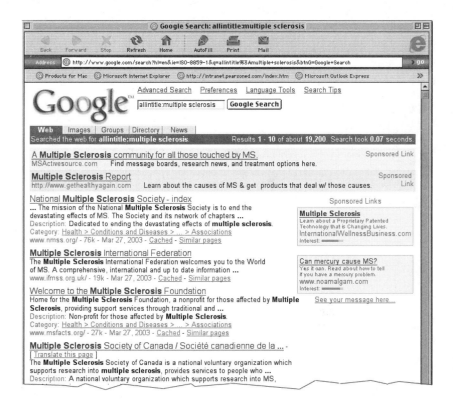

Online Databases

Much of the World Wide Web is not directly searchable from most search engines--the information is so specialized or constantly changing that it is "invisible" to the software that search engines use to access databases. These databases are often referred to as the "invisible Web" or "deep Web." Yet information stored in these databases is accessible if you know how to find it.

Some search engines and portals help by offering separate search options for the kinds of dynamically changing information, such as job listings and news, that search engines normally can't find. Yahoo's HotJobs (hotjobs.yahoo.com) and Google's news site (news.google.com) are examples of specialized search functions separate from the company's main search engine. Some sites also offer search options for multimedia and image files (Google's Image Search), and files created in non-standard file types such as Portable Document Format (PDF).

There are websites that specialize in collecting links to databases available on the Web. One such site is called The Invisible Web (www.invisibleweb.com) and links to 10,000 Web-accessible databases.

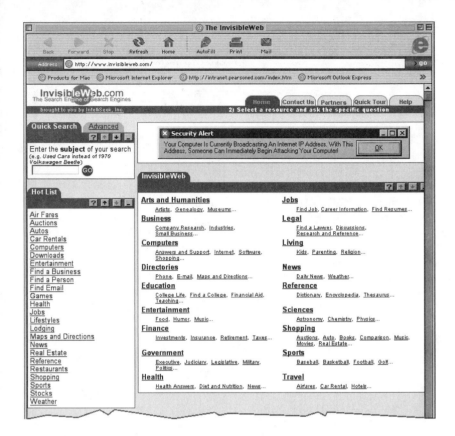

You may also want to visit other sites that collect links to Web databases:

- **Resource Discovery Network**   www.rdn.ac.uk
- **ProFusion**   www.profusion.com
- **Complete Planet**   www.completeplanet.com
- **Geniusfind**   geniusfind.com

Strategies for Searching Online Databases

Google and other search engines can locate searchable databases by searching a subject term and the word "database." For example, type **aviation accidents database** in Google, and you will get thousands of results, including a federal government database with information from 1962 and later about civil aviation accidents in the United States.

16

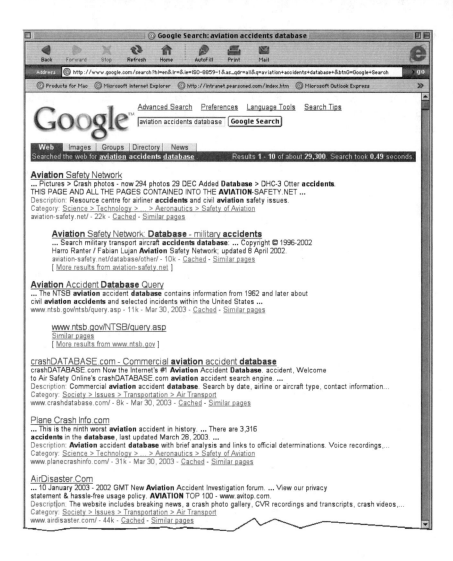

The word **database** is also helpful in searching a topic in Yahoo!, because Yahoo! uses the term to describe searchable databases in its listings. Examples:

- U.S. presidential election results database
- languages database
- toxic chemicals database

Such databases, especially if they are sponsored by government sites (identified by the **.gov** at the end of the URL), can be extremely useful as primary sources.

Planning a Search Strategy

The University of California at Berkeley has come up with a checklist (http://www.lib.berkeley.edu/TeachingLib/Guides/Internet/Strategies.html) to help you plan your search strategy. The first step is to analyze your topic to decide where to begin. Then you pick the right starting point depending on your analysis:

- If it has a distinctive word or phrase ("Battle of Gettysburg"), enclose the phrase in double quotation marks and test-run it in Google. Or search the broader concept in a subject directory.

- If it has *no* distinctive words or phrases, use more than one term or a phrase in double quotes to get fewer results from a search engine. Or try to find distinctive terms in subject directories.

- If you want an overview ("energy conservation"), look for a specialized subject directory on your topic.

- If you're seeking a narrow aspect of a broad or common topic (the role of governors in death-row pardons), try AltaVista's advanced search (www.altavista.com) or look for a directory focused on the broad subject (capital punishment).

- If your topic has synonyms (sea lion or pinniped), equivalent terms (energy conservation or fuel conservation), variant spellings (Thelonious Monk or Thelonius Monk), or endings that need to be included, choose engines with Boolean logic or truncation.

- If you don't even know where to start--you're confused and need more information--look for a gateway page or subject guide (Research Navigator's Link Library, www.researchnavigator.com), try an encyclopedia in a virtual library (the Internet Public Library, www.ipl.org), or ask at a library reference desk.

Then, stay flexible: learn as you go and vary your approach with what you learn. Don't get bogged down in a strategy that doesn't work. Switch from search engines to directories and vice versa. Find specialized directories on your topic and possible databases.

Evaluating Online Sources

In your career as a student and eventually as a professional, you will spend a great deal of time using the Internet to communicate and find information. But can you trust the information you find?

Suppose you come across two arguments regarding the greenhouse gas effect and global warming. Here are the views of a scientist who believes there is little or no greenhouse gas effect:

> Although thermometers located at Earth's surface indicate that the planet's average temperature is higher today by about 1°F than it was 140 years ago, satellite measurements of the temperature of the atmosphere thousands of feet above the surface indicate little or no warming since 1979. The difference between temperatures aloft and at the surface is not predicted by computer climate models. Therefore these models cannot be relied upon to project future warming, and the surface warming itself may be an artifact caused by urban heat islands rather than a true global warming trend.

Here is the response of an environmental organization that believes global warming is human-caused and a real threat to the environment:

> The method of translation of the satellite data into temperatures has been revised several times as errors were found and it is still not clear that these data provide a reliable means to determine long term trends. At higher altitudes, temperatures fluctuate more than at the surface due to natural climate influences like sunlight-reflecting particles from volcanoes. This variability or noise in the satellite record obscures the warming trend due to the buildup of the greenhouse gases, which is apparent in the global surface temperature data.

Which is more credible, the dissident scientist or the environmental organization? The organization also cites scientific research to back up its arguments. Because experts disagree, we need to consider the source.

Criteria for Evaluating Online Sources

How do you know which authorities and online sources to trust? When you look for information, you need to know the basis of the author's authority. Here are some questions you can ask to answer the question: How dependable is the source?

- Is the authority well-known and well-regarded?

- What are the authority's credentials (position, institutional affiliation)? You can check the Web page for a biography, check links to other documents, or check the author's homepage.

- Was the authority in a position to have access to pertinent facts? Someone who was a firsthand observer of the events in question is usually (but not always) more reliable. In general, primary sources are more impressive than secondary sources.

- Has the authority been screened by some organization? For example, articles in academic journals are evaluated by peers--experts in the field--to help determine if they should be accepted for publication.

- What are the likely biases? Factors that can influence how evidence is reported are personal needs, prior expectations, general beliefs, attitudes, values, theories, and ideologies. Few experts are without bias, but some have less bias than others. We can try to determine that bias by seeking information about the authority's personal interest in the topic of discussion. We need to be especially wary if an authority stands to benefit financially from the actions he or she advocates.

- How scholarly and fair has the author been? Does the author show knowledge of related sources, with appropriate citations? If claims need empirical support, does the author provide research evidence? If the topic is controversial, does the author acknowledge this and present several sides of the issue, or is the presentation one-sided? Does the document include a full biography, with references to high-quality sources, including primary sources and recent scholarly reviews? Is the information recent and up-to- date?

- Is the information timely and up-to-date? When was it produced and last updated?

Differences Among Sources of Information on the Web

The motives and purposes of those who put up websites vary greatly, and those differences affect the quality of the information. To determine the likely motives of website sponsors, you need to know who the sponsors are. Try to determine the following about any site you are using for information:

- The name of the organization or individual responsible.
- Links to additional information about the organization or individual.
- A clear statement of the site's goals.
- A clear indication of any financial sponsors and whether they are profit or nonprofit.

Your next question is: What are the likely motives of the source? Some possibilities:

- **To inform.** Many websites exist simply to present information on a topic. URL addresses that end in **.edu** or **.gov** tend to be informational because they are sponsored by educational institutions or by government agencies. Some examples: Library of Congress (lcweb.loc.gov), U.S. Environmental Protection Agency (www.epa.gov), the Internet Encyclopedia of Philosophy (www.utm.edu/research/iep/) and the U.S. Department of Commerce (www.commerce.gov).

- **To advocate.** The purpose of an advocacy page is to persuade you. Such pages reflect strong biases, which you need to identify in judging the quality of the information. URL addresses often end in .org if they are sponsored by a nonprofit organization. If a site's authors and sponsors seek financial donations, promote a cause, try to recruit members to an organization or provide ways for like-mind people to pursue further contact, it is an advocacy page. Organizations like Planned Parenthood, the National Rifle Association, the National Organization for Women, the Christian Coalition, and the ACLU sponsor advocacy sites.

- **To sell.** The primary purpose of many websites is to promote or sell products or services; you need to be especially alert to biases in information from such sites. URL addresses whose purpose is to sell often end in **.com**. Examples: Amazon.com, Ebay, the Gap, and Circuit City.

- **To provide news.** Many of these sites are postings of news from traditional print sources such as *The New York Times*, *USA Today*, *Newsweek*, and *Time*. Some news sites (Slate.com and Salon.com, for example) gather information from and link to multiple news sites as well as providing their own content.

- **To express individual opinions.** Many websites are created by individuals who want to express themselves. They may take the form of online journals, art galleries, or poetry sites. Web logs, called "blogs," whose authors comment on issues and link to news sites or like-minded Web authors, are increasingly popular. Personal opinion Web pages are very diverse and often very biased. Find out as much as you can about the person behind the site to decide how much credence to give his or her opinions.

- **Mixed motives.** Websites often reflect multiple motives. Be especially alert to sites that suggest one motive (information) but actually reflect other important motives (such as selling). An example is the "teen health" site listed on Yahoo! that is sponsored by a men's magazine--it blankets the site with advertising for health products. Another common practice is to make a website look as though it is informing when it is also advocating. If you are writing a paper on gun control, you may want to review sites sponsored by both pro- and anti-gun groups, but keep in mind their biases before you use any information from them.

Omitted Information

The information that you find at any particular site is selective. There are limitations imposed by time and space. Readers have limited attention spans and the communicator's knowledge is always incomplete. Sometimes, an author means to deceive: advertisers omit information that reflects badly on their products, and experts sometimes leave out information that would weaken their arguments. Finally, people have different values, beliefs, and attitudes. An individual's perspective may prevent him from noting information presented by those with different perspectives.

To get a fair picture of an issue or make a sound judgment on a research question, you need to pursue the omitted information. As you read a document, ask yourself questions to help you fill in what is missing:

- **Counterarguments.** What reasons would someone who disagrees offer? Are there research studies that contradict the studies presented? Are there missing examples that support the other side of the argument?

- **Definitions.** How would the arguments differ if key terms were defined in other ways?

- **Value preferences or perspectives.** From what other set of values might one approach this issue?

- **Origins of "facts" alluded to in the argument.** Are the factual claims supported by well-done research or by reliable sources?

- **Process used for gathering facts.** Was a survey conducted scientifically? How were respondents chosen and how were questions worded?

- **Figures, graphs, and data.** Would statistical results look different if they included evidence from different years? Have figures been selected to make a stronger case?

- **Effects of what is advocated or opposed.** What are the proposal's impacts, positive and negative, short- and long-term? Could there be unintended consequences? Which segments of society would gain and which would lose? What about other impacts: political, economic, biological, spiritual, health, interpersonal, or environmental?

- **Benefits accruing to the author.** Will the author benefit financially if we adopt his or her proposal?

Of course, reasoning is always incomplete. You could never form an opinion if you believed you had to find every possible piece of information on the subject first. But you can improve your arguments and your writing by gathering the most reliable and current information possible, given your limitations of time and space.

Chapter 3

Avoiding Plagiarism and Using Sources Ethically

What Is Plagiarism?

It is plagiarism to present another person's words or ideas as if they were your own. A kind of theft, plagarism can result in failing a course or even in expulsion from college. While blatant, intentional plagiarism is not the campus norm, many students fail to fully understand what constitutes plagiarism. Internet research in particular poses pitfalls: information can be copied from the Web with the click of a mouse, and too many students wrongly believe that anything on the Internet is in the public domain (see the section "Using Copyrighted Materials" at the end of this chapter). Others believe that they can escape detection because a professor couldn't read all the possible sources on a topic; however, instructors can now access websites that scan documents and search the Internet to identify plagiarized material.

The most flagrant forms of plagiarism are the use of another student's work, the purchase of a "canned" research paper, or knowingly copying passages into a research paper without documentation. Sometimes students unintentionally plagiarize through carelessness--by leaving off quotation marks or failing to document sources properly. Also, too many students believe that merely changing sentence order or a few words in a passage avoids plagiarism.

How to Avoid Plagiarism

Always credit the source for any ideas and words not your own. That said, a fear of plagiarism should not force you to document the obvious. You do not have to document common knowledge--information that most educated people know. (For example, that George W. Bush did not win the popular vote in the 2000 presidential election is common knowledge; a newspaper citation would be unnecessary.) You also do not have to document your own thinking, including points or conclusions that you have reached through the course of your research.

Paraphrasing

When you paraphrase, you restate *in your own words* a passage written or spoken by another person--and no more. Your writing should reflect the original passage's emphasis in your own phrasing and sentence structure. Compare the following passages. Here's the original, from a Stanford University website on South Africa:

> With the enactment of apartheid laws in 1948, racial discrimination was institutionalized. Race laws touched every aspect of social life, including a prohibition of marriage between non-whites and whites, and the sanctioning of "white-only" jobs. In 1950, the Population Registration Act required that all South Africans be racially classified into one of three categories, white, black (African) or colored (of mixed descent). The colored category included major subgroups of Indians and Asians. Classification into these categories was based on appearance, social acceptance and descent. For example, a white person was defined as "in appearance obviously a white person or generally accepted as a white person." A person could not be considered white if one of his or her parents were non-white. The determination that a person was "obviously white" would take into account "his habits, education and speech, and deportment and demeanor" (Chokshi, Carter, Gupta, Martin, & Allen, 1991).

Unacceptable Paraphrase (underlined words are plagiarized):

> According to Chokshi et al. (1991), <u>racial discrimination was institutionalized</u> with passage of the apartheid laws in 1948. <u>Race laws touched every aspect of social life</u>, including banning marriage between races, and the <u>sanctioning of "white-only" jobs</u>. The 1950 Population Registration Act <u>required that all South Africans be racially classified as white, black (African) or colored (of mixed descent,</u> Indian or Asian). Classification <u>was based on appearance, social acceptance and descent</u>. A white person, for example, was "in appearance obviously a white person or generally accepted as a white person." <u>A person could not be considered white if one of his parents were non-white</u>. According to the act, determining <u>that a person was "obviously white"</u> <u>would take into account</u> "his habits, education and speech, and deportment and demeanor.

In the above example, citing the authors (Chokshi et al., meaning "Chokshi and others") at the beginning does not legitimize using the authors' exact wording-- nor does changing a few words and the order of phrases.

Acceptable Paraphrase:

> The 1948 apartheid laws made racial discrimination official. The wide-ranging laws allowed "white-only" jobs and banned marriage between races. Two years later, the Population Registration Act classified all South Africans into one of three racial categories: white, black

(African) or colored. "Colored" South Africans were of mixed descent or were Indians or Asians. According to Chokshi et al. (1991), the categories were determined by "appearance, social acceptance and descent." An officially "white" person, then, had been judged to look like a white person or was accepted as one. A white person could not have a non-white parent. The act posited that "habits, education and speech, and deportment and demeanor" would help determine the classification.

Here, the writer has borrowed two phrases from the original, but enclosed them in quotes or attributed them properly--to Chokshi et al. and the Population Registration Act.

Summarizing

A summary condenses the essentials of someone else's thought into a few statements. A summary is shorter than a paraphrase and provides only the main point from the original source. Keep it short; a summary should reduce the original by at least half. As with a paraphrase, keep your own ideas and opinions separate; you may want to note them to yourself and use them elsewhere in your paper, however.

Here is how the above quotation could be summarized:

The 1948 apartheid laws institutionalized racial discrimination in South Africa, affecting all aspects of social life. The 1950 Population Registration Act set up three categories of races, determined by such factors as appearance and descent (Chokshi, Carter, Gupta, Martin & Allen, 1991).

How to Include Reference Citations in Your Text

As you take notes, keep meticulous track of your sources. You may want to print a hard copy of each Web article used in order to save the author or authors, organization, title, date and URL for later reference--especially since Web pages are created and taken down constantly. Find out which documentation standard your instructor is using. The major styles used are MLA (Modern Language Association), APA (American Psychological Association), CMS (Chicago Manual of Style), or CBE (Council of Biology Editors, now the Council of Science Editors). All of these styles may be found on the Research Navigator homepage (www.researchnavigator.com) at the "Citing Your Sources" tab.

Here's how the entry on your "Works Cited" page would look for the apartheid quote using APA style:

Monal Chokshi, Cale Carter, Deepak Gupta, Tove Martin & Robert Allen (1991). Computers and the apartheid regime in South Africa. *South Africa. Guide to Internet Resources. Stanford University.* Retrieved Dec. 12, 2002, from the World Wide Web: http://www-cs-students.stanford.edu/~cale/cs201

In the example above, the authors' names are followed by the year the paper was written, the paper's title, and the name of the website (in italics). The date it was retrieved is followed by the URL. If the source is from a journal, you'll need to include the title of the periodical or electronic text, volume number, and pages.

The process for citing a Web source within text is similar to citing a print source. Within your text, you will need to provide enough information to identify a source with a name or website. If the site includes page numbers or paragraph numbers, use those as well. (In subsequent references to the same authority, the author's last name is usually sufficient.) Keep citations brief; you will fully document each source on the "Works Cited" page. If no author is listed, use the article title or website information for your in-text citation:

> South Africa's minority government used technology--especially computer hardware and software--as a tool of repression (*Computers and the Apartheid Regime in South Africa,* 1991).

Quoting Sources

Direct quotations from online material follow the same rules as non-Internet material. Enclose within quotations marks all quoted materials--a phrase, a sentence, a paragraph. (Some documentation styles specify that if you are quoting more than a sentence or two, the quote should be indented instead and set off typographically.)

Don't load a paper with quotations; if more than a quarter of your essay consists of quotations, you are letting others speak for you and giving the impression that you have not synthesized the material. When drawing from an authority, rely mostly on paraphrase and summary. *Do* use a quotation, however, when it fits your message and its language is particularly on point or if the idea is hard to paraphrase accurately.

> Diane Sollee (1996), the founder and director of the Coalition for Marriage, Family and Couples Education, said, "The number one predictor of divorce is the habitual avoidance of conflict."

Quote exactly; if you drop a quoted phrase within a sentence, make sure the grammar meshes with your own. If you eliminate a sentence or words within the quote, use ellipses according to the appropriate documentation style.

Halberstam (2001) described "... a dramatically changed America, one which has been challenged by the cruelest kind of terrorism, and which is in a kind of suspended state between war and peace ...and where so much of our normal agenda has been brushed aside."

Using Copyrighted Materials

Just as a patent protects an inventor's rights to exploit a new product, a copyright signifies original creation and ownership of written words, music, or images. As a student, you may use copyrighted material in your research paper under the doctrine of fair use, which allows the use of others' words for such informational purposes as criticism, comment, news reporting, teaching, scholarship, or research. Academic integrity requires documenting such use in the manner covered in this chapter.

Copyright law is not intended to halt the flow of ideas and facts; it is meant to protect the literary, musical, or visual form that an author or artist uses to express his concepts. For example, there is a popular poem called "Warning" by Jenny Joseph (1961) that begins, "When I am an old woman I shall wear purple/ With a red hat which doesn't go and doesn't suit me." Several websites publish a shorter, adapted version of the poem, but anyone who wants a full version is directed to buy products from a company that has bought publishing rights to the poem. If anyone could sell products displaying Joseph's poem, its value to Joseph and the authorized publisher would be greatly diminished. Few artworks are as commercial as this, but a literary critic who published, without permission, all seven lines of a seven-line poem in her review would be violating copyright law as well. In either case, it *is* permissible to describe the ideas and facts contained in a work or quote brief passages; what is *not* permissible is to copy or reprint large portions of the work in its original literary, musical, or visual format without permission.

If you use substantial blocks of material, or you want to download images for your paper, you should seek permission from the author or website. When in doubt, consult your instructor or e-mail the author or another contact for the Internet site.

27

Chapter 4

Introducing
Research Navigator™

What Is Research Navigator
and How Can It Help with Research?

Research Navigator is an online academic research service that combines three major databases with practical research assistance--all in one place on the Web. It can help you understand the steps in the research process while also providing in-depth information on conducting library research.

Research Navigator offers these databases of credible and reliable source material: EBSCO's ContentSelect Academic Journal and Abstract Database, The *New York Times* Search by Subject Archive, and "Best of the Web" Link Library. It also guides students step-by-step through the writing of a research paper. Access to Research Navigator is free with the purchase of any Pearson Education college textbook.

To begin using Research Navigator, register with the personal access code found in this *Guide to Online Research*. Once you register, you have access to all the resources in Research Navigator for six months.

What's in Research Navigator?

From the homepage, you can gain access to all of the site's main features, including the three databases--for academic journals and general interest publications (EBSCO's ContentSelect), newspaper articles (The *New York Times* Search by Subject Archive), and World Wide Web sites ("Best of the Web" Link Library)--that will be discussed in greater detail later. If you are new to the research process, you may want to start by browsing "Understanding the Research Process," located in the upper right-hand section of the homepage. Here you will find help on all aspects of conducting research, from gathering data to searching the Internet, evaluating sources, drafting the paper, and revising and editing the final draft.

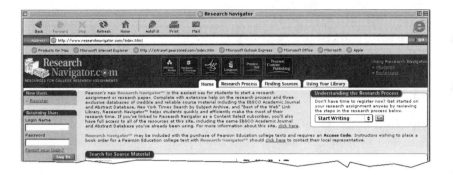

ContentSelect

EBSCO's ContentSelect Research Database gives you instant access to thousands of academic journals and periodicals from any computer with an Internet connection.

When you need the most authoritative take on a subject, especially one that is complex or very specialized, you will turn to academic journals. Academic journals are aimed at a professional audience--researchers, instructors, and experts, usually affiliated with colleges and universities. Academic-journal articles have been peer-reviewed before publication; that is, they have been checked for balance, methodology, and significance by other experts in the field. An article that doesn't meet the profession's standards will not be published in an academic journal. Examples of academic journals are *Science, Nature, American Ethnologist, Journal of Chemical Education*, and *Canadian Journal of Sociology*.

When you do a search, your list will include some results in full-text format. The full article may be in HTML, the common language used to write Web documents, or it may be in a PDF format. PDF is a file format that creates high-resolution documents; to read such documents, however, you need to first download a free viewer, Adobe Acrobat Reader.

Many ContentSelect results will be in a citation format; when you click on those results, you will get a biblographic reference with author, subject, and journal source. A citation will usually contain an abstract, or brief summary of the article, that will help you determine whether you want to find the full article. You then find the full article through the journal's online archive, or in a print or electronic version through your college library's catalog.

To use ContentSelect, select a database to search and then enter a keyword. For more detailed information, see Chapter 7.

The *New York Times*
Search by Subject Archive

Among daily newspapers, the *New York Times* is the gold standard. It is widely considered the nation's newspaper of record because it is comprehensive and staffed by reporters and editors who are experienced and well-regarded. It has substantial resources and a tradition of excellence.

The *Times*, however, like other newspapers, is aimed at a general audience and is limited by daily deadlines, competitive pressures, and space, so individual articles may not be suitable sources for a complex or very specialized research topic. But for day-to-day coverage of events and popular issues, and general, accessible background information on a wide range of topics, it is first rate.

Research Navigator gives you access to a one-year archive of articles from the *New York Times*. The archives are searchable by subject and by keyword. For tips on how to use the *New York Times* archive, see Chapter 5. Articles can be printed or saved for later use in your research assignment. Be sure to review the rules for citing a newspaper article in endnotes or a bibliography.

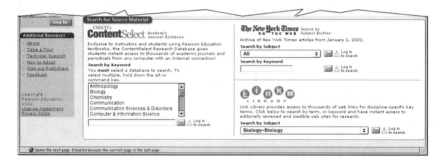

Link Library

Link Library is a collection of links to websites, organized by academic subject and key terms. To use this database, select a subject from the drop-down list. You will be taken to a list of key terms; find the key term for your subject and see a list of five or more editorially reviewed websites that offer educationally relevant and credible content. The Web links in Link Library are monitored and updated each week, reducing your chances of encountering dead links.

Other Resources within Research Navigator

Using Your Library

Despite the Internet revolution, a visit to a bricks-and-mortar library continues to be an important part of the research process. Use the drop-down list on the

Research Navigator homepage "Using Your Library" tab to select a "Library Guide" for your subject. The guide will list Library of Congress and Dewey call numbers, major print and online journals, organizations and associations, discussion lists, and Internet resources. Print it out and take it with you to help you navigate a library's vast resources more efficiently.

"Using Your Library" also discusses types of libraries, their resources, how to choose which ones to use, and the research process and how to develop a timeframe for it.

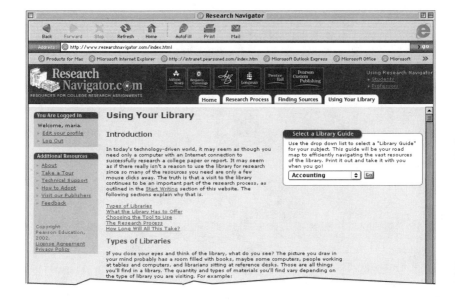

The Research Process

There are several key steps to the research process, beginning with the selection of a research topic and the development of a tentative thesis. The three hyperlinked sections under the "Research Process" tab--"Start Writing," "Internet Research," and "Citing Sources"--explain the research process in greater detail, including how to evaluate good source material, how to properly cite sources, and how to develop endnotes or a bibliography.

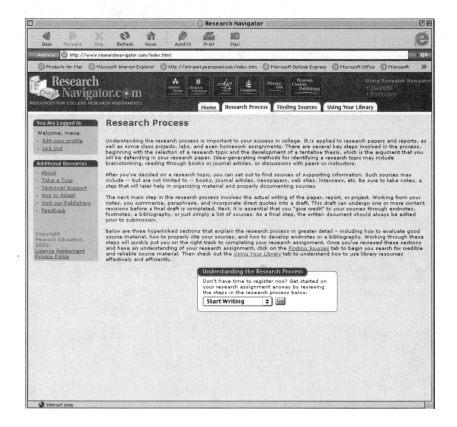

Finding Sources

This section of Research Navigator helps start your search for credible and reliable source material by offering three databases of source material, similar to those offered by a library. EBSCO's Academic Journal and Abstract Database gives you journal articles from leading academic journals as well as articles from many leading popular periodicals, such as *Newsweek* and *USA Today*. The *New York Times* Search by Subject Archive lets you review newspaper articles from the past year, and Link Library points you to the "Best of the Web" sites that have been screened for educational relevance to key topics.

If you need more source material, or are ready to go to the library to conduct a more detailed and thorough search, click on "Using Your Library" and review suggestions for making the most of your time at the library.

Chapter 5

Using the *New York Times* Search by Subject Archive

About the *New York Times*

Newspapers, also known as periodicals because they are issued in periodic installments (e.g. daily, weekly, or monthly), provide contemporary information. Although they don't have the scholarly authority of academic journals, newspapers are often the best source of the latest information on popular and controversial topics. Political struggles, economic debates, election campaigns and issues, scientific advances, the arts and contemporary social trends are all extensively covered by periodicals.

Research Navigator gives you access to a search-by-subject archive of articles from one of the world's leading newspapers: the *New York Times*. Since its founding in 1851, the *New York Times* has become the nation's newspaper of record--the publication that other media look to as a guide for coverage and responsible news judgment. The *Times* is still the leader among news organizations in winning Pulitzer Prizes, journalism's top award, with 108 prizes through 2002. It employs more than 1,000 editors, reporters, photographers, artists, and designers in its news department. Its reach is truly global: in 2001, the *Times* had 30 reporters in Washington, D.C.; 30 reporters in U.S. bureaus outside Washington and New York; and 40 staff correspondents and contributors in 26 news bureaus around the world.

Using the criteria we established in Chapter 2 for the dependability of sources, the *Times*:

- is well-known and well-regarded.
- has impressive credentials (Pulitzer Prizes, experienced reporters and editors).
- has access to pertinent facts (numerous correspondents provide firsthand accounts worldwide).

On the other hand, *Times* content is not peer-reviewed in the way that an academic journal is. Its content *is* screened informally by media observers and critics who are quick to pounce on any perceived errors or biases. In recent years, questions have been raised about the *Times'* coverage of a cancer "breakthrough," an Asian-American scientist suspected of being a spy, and attendance at anti-Iraq-war rallies. When *Times* editors have been convinced that criticisms have merit, they have published follow-up stories or editor's notes acknowledging errors of fact or emphasis. When smaller factual errors come to light, the *Times*, like most leading newspapers, prints timely corrections; some online archives, such as LexisNexis, append the corrections to the story.

So, while the *Times* is an excellent source for information on current topics, keep in mind that it has daily deadlines, competitive pressures, and fallible editors and reporters--like all newspapers. You need to apply the same skepticism toward the information it provides as you would with any other source. Check factual claims with other sources and be alert for signs of bias and omitted information.

What's in the Archive?

Research Navigator's *New York Times* archive organizes articles published in the past year by more than 135 academic subjects, from accounting to zoology. It only includes articles deemed relevant and timely for research; you will not find recipes or wedding announcements. The *Times* archive contents are updated every day.

The *Times'* regular website, www.nytimes.com, contains the full content of the print edition as well as additional articles and images. The newspaper's own archive includes articles from as far back as January 1, 1996, but at the time this guide was written, the *Times* charged a fee to access articles--except for art, book, and entertainment reviews--that were more than seven days old.

When and How to Use *New York Times* Articles

If you want to know the latest on an issue or breaking news story, check Research Navigator's *New York Times* archive. Want to know the status of congressional action regarding offshore income-tax shelters? What are the most recent developments with charter schools? What are the two political parties' stands on affirmative action? Go to the relevant subject directory, or do a keyword search, or both.

But if you are researching existential philosophers, European colonialism in the Congo, or the photography of Walker Evans, for example, a newspaper archive is not the place to start. For non-contemporary subjects, especially complex academic topics, you should consider academic journals, subject directories, and search engines for finding online sources. Research Navigator's ContentSelect and Link Library, which are explained in the next two chapters, will help you find directories and search engines more suited to your topic.

Searching the Archive

Search by Subject

Searching the *New York Times* archive by subject is not only easy, it's also more suited to browsing than to finding a specific topic. The "constitutional law" grouping had 166 articles when this was written, and the "American government" heading had nearly 4,000. But once you have called up a subject area, you are taken to an advanced search page and you can further refine your search with a keyword or words. Articles can be printed or saved for later use. Be sure to review the citation rules for how to cite a newspaper article in endnotes or a bibliography.

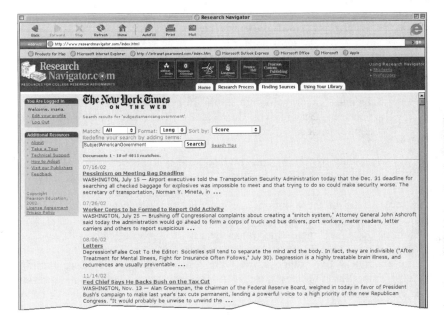

Search by Keyword

Type a word, or multiple words separated by commas, into the search box. If you are using more than one word, there are three **match** options for you to choose from.

- The "All" option will pull up all articles with all of the key terms you enter as well as their various word endings. So, for example, if you search for articles with the words **Enron** and **auditor**, your search results will include articles that contain the words **Enron** and **auditor** as well as articles that contain the words **Enron** and **auditors**.

- The "Any" option is equivalent to the Boolean "or." It will pull up all articles with any of the terms you enter. Using the same key words as above, **Enron** and **auditor**, the "any" option will yield articles that contain the words **Enron** or **auditor** or **auditors**.

- The "Boolean" option lets you use the Boolean operators "and," "or," and "not" to refine your search. See Chapter 2 for more information on using Boolean terms.

In addition, there are two **format** options: "Long" and "Short." The search results for the default, Long, will include headlines and the first five lines from each of the articles. The alternative, Short, will just list the article headlines.

Finally, there are six **sort by** options from which to choose.

- The default, "Score," presents search results in order of the number of times your key words appear in the articles. "Reverse Score" does just the opposite: it lists search results from those articles with the fewest mentions of your key terms first.

- Selecting "Time" will yield results from the most recent to the oldest articles in the archive. Conversely, "Reverse Time" results are presented from oldest to most recent.

- Searching by "Title" will produce articles in alphabetical order based on the first word in the headline. "Reverse Title" will do the opposite.

The most useful of these options are probably the search by "Score," which ranks articles by the number of times they mention your search terms, and "Time" or "Reverse Time," which ranks the articles chronologically.

In the example above, suppose you were researching the role of accounting auditors in the Enron business scandal. At the time this was written, if you used the "Any" option for **Enron** and **auditor**, you'd get 2,708 results, many of them not useful because they included any article from the past year that mentioned "auditor" and any article that included "Enron." If you used the "All" option, you would get 481 results. You could also use the "sort by" options to make the list even more manageable, depending upon whether you wanted the most recent stories (select "Time") or the stories that have more mentions of your terms (select "Score"). If you want to narrow the results yet again, add another keyword. If you searched for **Enron**, **auditor**, and **Andersen** (for the accounting firm), you would get 343 matches. In addition, clicking on the "Long" form will let you read the headline and first paragraph of each article, but using the "Short" form, with headlines only, may help you scan results more quickly.

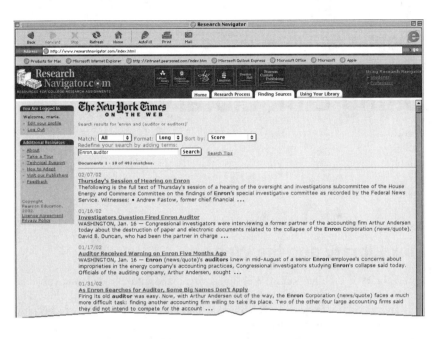

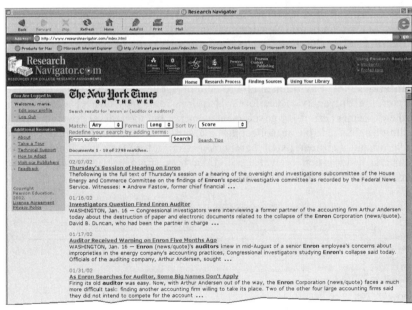

Chapter 6

Using Link Library

Link Library and the Web

Link Library is a collection of Web links, organized into 24 academic subjects, which are in turn divided into subcategories and lists of individual sites. The sites are editorially reviewed, which means that they have been selected because they offer credible and reliable information.

For example, if you were to select the "pollution" subcategory from the **Biology--Environmental Science** subject category, you would get a list of a dozen links. The site topics range from different types of pollution--air, noise, water--to the status of environmental legislation. How dependable are the sources? All are well-known and well-regarded government or educational institutions: the Environmental Protection Agency, NASA Ames Research Center, the University of California at Irvine. Some may quarrel with policies and enforcement efforts of government agencies, but the federal government has a long-established role in collecting data and disseminating information. The government websites listed here cover straightforward, non-controversial subjects: a definition of water pollution, how stratospheric ozone is being depleted, the latest city-by-city air pollution data, etc.

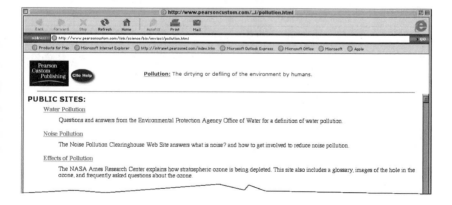

Suppose you look for the same information from websites listed by Yahoo! It turns out that many sites listed under "pollution" are from government and educational agencies. But you will also come across sites like one in which the author describes herself as "devoted to addressing the aspects of the environmental crisis left unacknowledged or inadequately addressed by the vast majority of existing environmental groups." The site is attractive, it doesn't solicit contributions, and it collects articles from generally well-regarded secondary sources, like the Associated Press. But its focus is on opinion, and lists topic headings such as "prophecy" and "prayer." It contains little of scholarly interest and no discernible research evidence. The site's author, while enthusiastic and well-intentioned, is not well-known or well-regarded.

In addition, the Web links in Research Navigator's Link Library are monitored and updated each week to reduce the chance of encountering "dead" links.

What's in Link Library?

Link Library echoes the variety of the World Wide Web. It offers images, text, government and academic documents and research, databases, and search engines. As with any subject directory, you need to narrow your search to the most useful category. You can find links to websites about AIDS, for example, in a half-dozen subject categories: biology, criminal justice, U.S. and world history, philosophy-ethics, and sociology. When you have selected a subject area and found the topic you are seeking, you will find a list of sites. The character of the site you choose to consult will often depend on your topic. The sites in Link Library can be:

- **Scholarly.** If you are researching photosynthesis and you go to the **Biology** subject area, you will find such sites as "What Is Photosynthesis?" and "Photosynthesis Research," maintained by Arizona State University. "Virtual Chloroplast," by the University of Illinois at Urbana-Champaign, contains an image of a chloroplast that lets you click on certain regions for more information.

- **Straightforward.** What if you want information on the 2000 presidential election but don't want to be flooded with opinion pieces about the disputed Florida results? Go to **Political Science – American Government > Presidential Elections**. It has sites such as "Atlas of U.S. Presidential Elections," with voting results for elections dating back to 1860; "U.S. Electoral College," the homepage for the National Archives and Records Administration Guide to the Electoral College; and "Elections," which provides graphs on electoral and popular votes for all U.S. presidential elections to date.

- **Controversial.** You're researching a topic that has heated arguments on both--or many--sides, and you want to summarize the range of public opinion. Link Library subject directories on such topics will lead you to a balanced variety of voices. Under **Philosophy–Ethics**, for example, you will find a list of "partial-birth abortion" links that include a pro-choice site, the text of the *Roe vs. Wade* decision, the National Right to Life Committee homepage, a site that attempts to provide all views of the issue, and a Planned Parenthood site that describes medical procedures performed at various stages of pregnancy.

- **Practical.** Want some help in finding sources on the Web? Go to the **Information Technology** subject directory. The "search engine" heading offers tips for effective Internet searching, common questions about how search engines work, and a chart to help you choose the best search engine for a task.

Finding Information with Link Library

To use this database, you choose a subject from the drop-down list, and, using the alphabetical directory, find the key term for the topic you are searching. Click on the key term and see a list of editorially reviewed websites.

Some topics with wide-ranging aspects appear under more than one subject heading. For example, a list of websites about alcoholism and alcohol abuse can be found under Criminal Justice, U.S. History, General Psychology, and Sociology.

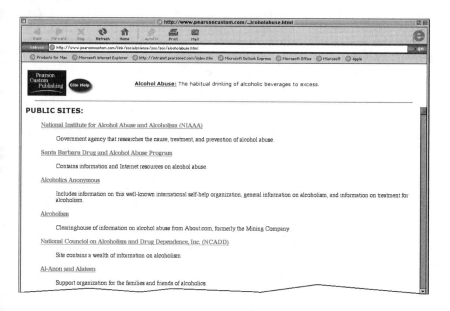

Chapter 7

Using ContentSelect

About ContentSelect

EBSCO's ContentSelect Academic Journal Database is an archive of scholarly peer-reviewed journals and general interest periodicals. Thousands of articles and citations from general interest publications and prestigious academic journals can be instantly accessed in several ways using ContentSelect's search engine. Titles are chosen to reflect multiple perspectives in a range of topics, under 22 broad subject headings in the sciences, humanities, and social sciences.

Of course, ContentSelect is not a substitute for evaluation. Careful research studies sometimes contradict one another, and even authorities disagree. However, while many sources on the Internet may present questionable data or rely on dubious authorities to draw conclusions, ContentSelect provides a wealth of professionally-reviewed information that you can search and evaluate with confidence.

What's in ContentSelect?

ContentSelect offers searchable databases of academic journals and general interest publications. Academic journals are peer-reviewed; general interest publications are not.

Academic Journals

Rather than having a staff of writers who write something on assignment, journals accept submissions from academic researchers all over the country and the world. The journal editor then relies on "peer reviewers," or experts in the author's field, to evaluate the papers submitted to help determine if they should be published. The result is that the content of journal articles meets a higher standard than that of popular magazines, newspaper articles or Web pages. Journals provide specialized knowledge and information about a research topic and adhere to strict professional guidelines for methodology and theoretical grounding.

Scholarly journals are published several times per year. All the issues published in one calendar year constitute a volume. For example, the *American Sociological Review*, the journal of the American Sociological Association, published Volume 65 in the year 2000. That year's volume was made up of six individual issues, numbered Vol. 65 No. 1 and so on.

Additionally, journal issues may contain letters to the editor, book reviews, and comments from authors.

General Interest Publications

In addition to scholarly journals, subject databases--particularly the General Interest database--in ContentSelect include periodicals that are not peer reviewed. Some examples are *Commentary*, *Washington Monthly*, *Newsweek*, *USA Today Magazine*, and the *Christian Science Monitor*. These publications are included because they have articles that are generally credible and reliable. If your topic is timely or controversial, general interest publications may offer more appropriate coverage than academic journals.

Sometimes it's not easy to know at first glance which category a publication fits. For example, you find an article in *Science News*. Is that an academic journal, as the journal *Science* is? When you go to your subject database, click on the "publications" tab. You can scroll down to *Science News* or use the "browse" button to find it. When you click on *Science News*, you'll get an information box that describes the subjects it covers plus a characterization of its content: "presents articles of interest to scientists and others ..." The "and others" is a clue; then, when you check the "peer reviewed" section, it has an "N" for "no." So *Science News* is a general interest publication, not an academic journal. Still, any article in *Science News* is probably reliable, subject to the evaluation you conduct for all sources (see Chapter 2).

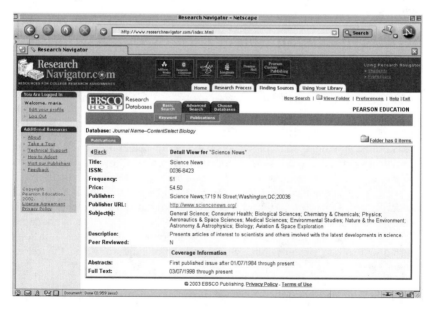

Searching ContentSelect

Select a Database

ContentSelect's homepage features a list of databases. To search within a single database, click the name of the database. To search in more than one database, hold down the alt or command key while clicking on the name of the database.

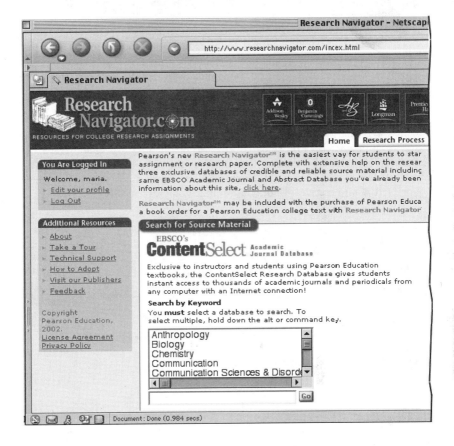

Basic Search

After selecting one or more databases, you must enter a keyword or keywords, then click on "go." This will take you to the basic search window. If you've selected a precise and distinctive keyword, your search may be done. But if you have too many results--which is often the case--you need to narrow your search.

The basic search window lets you create a search using a variety of search methods. Enter your search terms in the **Find** field and select from the available search modes: **standard**, **all words**, **any words**, or **exact phrase**.

Standard Search (Boolean)

- **And** combines search terms so that each result contains all of the terms. For example, search **SUV and conservation** to find only articles that contain both terms.

- **Or** combines search terms so that each result contains at least one of the terms. For example, search **SUV or conservation** to find results that contain either term.

- **Not** excludes terms so that each result does not contain the term that follows the "not" operator. For example, search **SUV not conservation** to find results that contain the term **SUV** but not the term **conservation.**

Using the above examples, suppose you were writing a paper about sport utility vehicles and energy conservation, in light of growing criticism of their low gasoline mileage. If you selected the "General Interest" database from ContentSelect and used the Boolean "or," at the time this was written, you would get 800 results for **SUV or conservation**. If you used the Boolean "and" option, (**SUV and conservation**) you would get only two results:

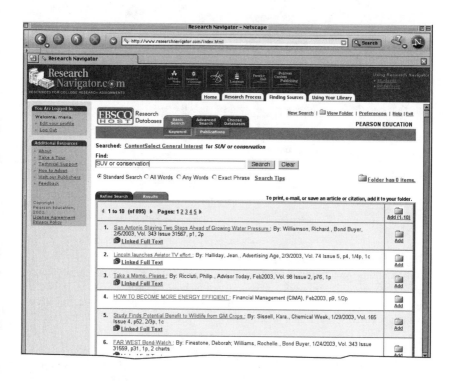

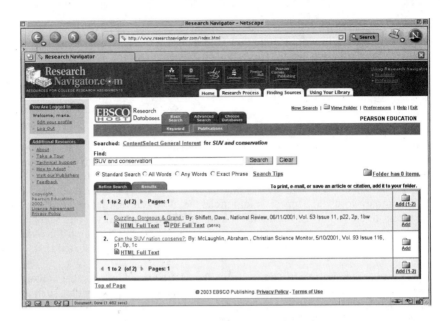

But suppose you decided to write about SUVs and didn't want articles that mentioned the energy conservation issue. If you searched for **SUV not conservation**, you would get 197 results:

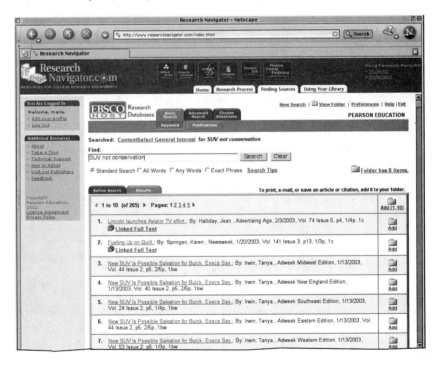

45

Using "All Words"

In the "All Words" mode, ContentSelect conducts a Boolean search, assuming an AND between each word. The order of the search words entered does not matter. Any results that are displayed must include all words entered, regardless of how close they are to each other. Your search results are presented in order by date.

Using "Any Words"

"Any words" will return pages that include at least one of your terms--equivalent to using the Boolean "or." For example, if you type in **SUV energy conservation,** you will get results that include one, two, or all three terms.

The more keywords that appear in an article, the more relevant the record is and the closer to the top of the results list it appears. What this means is that you can also enter a phrase or sentence that describes what you want to search for. Any results will appear in ranked order, with the most relevant article presented first.

For example, type **improving gas mileage for SUVs** to find articles that contain **improving, gas, mileage,** or **SUVs.** Prepositions such as **for** and articles such as **the** are excluded from the search. Results at the top of the list will have more (or all) of your keywords than results farther down the list.

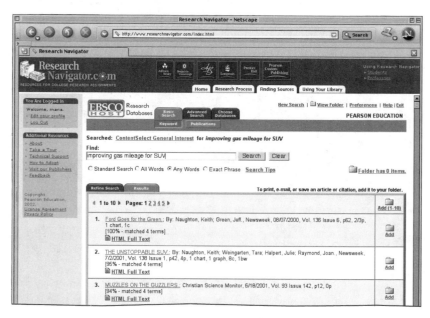

Using "Exact Phrase"

Enter the word or phrase that you want to find. Any results that are displayed will include all the words you entered, exactly as you entered them. (However, stop words--articles and prepositions--are still ignored.) Your search results are presented in order by date.

You can achieve the same results, clicking on any search method, by placing **quotation marks** around search terms. For example, type in **"gas mileage"** and click the "any words" option and you will get the same results you would by typing **gas mileage** and clicking the "exact phrase" option.

Advanced Search

On the tabbed tool bar, click **Advanced Search**. The advanced search window appears. Enter your search terms in the **Find** field. Your search terms can be keywords or selections from search history. Boolean operators (AND, OR, NOT) can also be included in your search.

You can also use **field codes** with your search terms. Fields refer to searchable aspects of an article or Web page; in the case of ContentSelect, they include author, title, subject, abstract, and journal name. Click **Field Codes** to display a list of field codes available with the databases you are using. Type the field code before your search terms to limit those words to the field you entered. For example, **AU Naughton** will find records that contain Naughton in the author field.

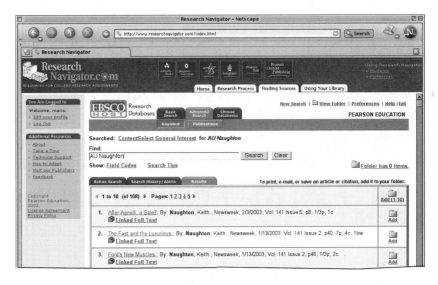

To **print, e-mail, or save** several search results, click on the folder next to the result; then print, e-mail, or save from the folder at the top of the results field. (You can still print, e-mail, or save individual results from the open article or citation.)

You can remove specific results, or clear the entire folder and collect new results, during your session. If you end your session, or it times out due to inactivity, the folder is automatically cleared.

Full Text Results

Some ContentSelect results will be available in full text--that is, if you click on the full text logo at the bottom of an entry, you will be able to call up the entire journal or magazine article. If you want to limit your search to results available in full text, click on the "search options" tab, and then on "full text." Then renew your search.

Abstract and Citation Results

Many ContentSelect results are in the form of citations containing abstracts. A **citation** is a bibliographic reference to an article or document, with basic information such as ISSN (International Standard Serial Number, the standard method for identifying publications) and publisher that will help you locate it. An **abstract** is a brief description of an article, usually written by the author. An abstract will help you decide whether you want to locate the work--either in an electronic database or a print version--through your college library.

A handy tip: once you have found an article that meets your research needs, you can search fields easily from the article citation to turn up similar articles. For example, suppose the *Christian Science Monitor* article "Gas-guzzling SUVs muster up a makeover" (Evarts, July 6, 2000) suits your paper perfectly. Go to the citation and click on the subject field to find similar articles. Or, if you want to see what else the author has written, click on the author field to produce a list of articles he has written.

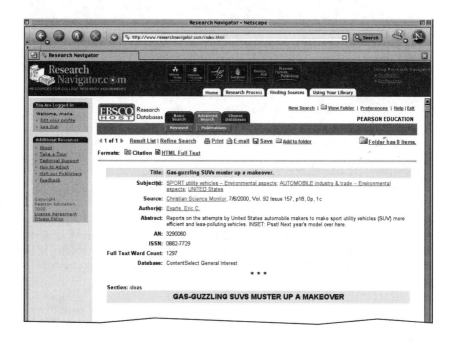

In many cases you can search the full text of articles using electronic databases and then read the entire article online. Typically, in order to use these databases you need to have a library card number or special password provided by the library. But sometimes when you use an electronic database you will find that the text of an article won't be accessible online, so you'll have to go to the library's shelves to find the magazine or newspaper in which the article originally appeared.

For more information, explore "Understanding the Research Process" and "Using Your Library" on the Research Navigator homepage.

Chapter 8

Writing a Research Paper Using Research Navigator and the World Wide Web

Research Assignment

As a college student, you will be asked to write research papers in many of your classes. It is important that you grow as a scholar and become comfortable with and adept at creating scholarly texts. This competence comes through practice, study, and reflection.

Instructors design research paper assignments to meet specific learning objectives, and these objectives will vary depending on the instructor's training and experience, the structure and requirements of the course, and the individual assignment. However, three objectives are present, to some degree, in all forms of research writing: first, instructors want you to develop skills in research and documentation; second, instructors want to challenge your reading skills by requiring you to summarize, analyze, and evaluate scholarly texts; and third, instructors want you to become part of the scholarly conversation through your research writing.

When you receive a research assignment, your first task is to be clear on the parameters of the paper and the expectations of your instructor. Ask questions in class and during office hours to be sure you understand the learning objectives of the paper as well as the specific requirements for the assignment. In order to start your research project, you need to be able to answer the following questions.

- **What is the minimum length for the paper?**
  The instructor will usually have clear expectations on the minimum length of your paper. Take this requirement seriously. If you find you need more space to complete your writing task, then you should discuss this with your instructor.

- **How many and what kinds of sources should be included in the body of the paper? What are the source requirements for the works cited?**
  The length of the paper is directly connected to the number of required sources. A common rule is to have two (2) citations (references to authoritative texts) per double-spaced page of text (250 words). For example, if you are asked to write a paper of 2500 words, approximately 10 pages, you will need roughly 20 in-text citations from a variety of sources including articles from scholarly journals, government documents, field research, etc. This is a general statement, so you will need to verify specifics with your instructor. Be clear on what the writing situation requires.
- **What citation format should I follow?**
  The answer to this question depends upon the discipline you are writing for: Modern Language Association (MLA) format is used in the humanities and in this text; American Psychological Association (APA) format is used in the social sciences; Council of Science Editors (CSE) format is used in mathematics, physical sciences, and life sciences. Always confirm the documentation style with your instructor.
- **What is the purpose of the paper?**
  The specific purpose of your individual paper will be determined as you research, read, prewrite, and draft, but your instructor may prescribe a general purpose: to inform or to persuade. An informative structure allows you to educate readers and present information in an objective manner. A persuasive structure allows you the opportunity to arrange evidence in such a way that your readers agree with (or at least accept) your position on your topic. Put another way, your persuasive paper should seek to engage an audience that disagrees with your claim (debatable thesis); at a minimum, readers should identify with your argument, and accept your position on the topic, but ideally, readers will agree with your position and change their thinking, behavior, or attitude. Ultimately, whether your paper is informative or persuasive, your goal should be for your readers to gain something out of your writing. If you only think about grades and getting done, you still need to develop this important characteristic of an essay because most instructors look for a strong sense of purpose when evaluating.
- **Is there an assigned topic?**
  Sometimes an instructor has specific content he or she wants you to learn, or maybe the class is studying an umbrella theme, so you may have an assigned topic. Occasionally, you may even be asked to write a research paper based on an assigned thesis statement—for the purpose of in-class debate or the like. If you have an umbrella theme or assigned topic, do not feel as though you are limited in your study or approach. You have a great deal of freedom to focus the topic in a way and area that interests you.

Finding a Topic

If you need to choose the topic, consider the assignment criteria as you decide. Certain topics are not compatible with certain requirements. For example, if you are to write an argumentative paper, finding a debatable claim is critical. While experienced rhetoricians may find an argument in just about any topic, undergraduate writers may find it difficult to find an argument in topics such as the history of Social Justice Theory, the food pyramid, or deciduous forests. So the purpose and length should be considerations as you think, discuss, and prewrite about your possible topic.

Try brainstorming in each of these topic categories: hobbies, your personal academic interests, your major, or current social or political events. Write for a limited time to create four lists, 5-10 minutes per category. Here's an example of brainstorming.

Hobbies	Academic Interests	Your Major	Current Events
Cars	Religion	Education-	U.S./Iraq
Vintage clothing	Philosophy	public funding	United Nations
Travel	Chinese culture	History-	International
Gardening	"How people	Interpreta-	Relations
Yoga	learn"	tion of an	War
Running	Constitution	event	Poverty
Weightlifting	Service	Spanish-	Crime
Music	Learning	Translation	Social
Cooking	research	strategies	Justice
Reading	Sudan's Civil War	Rhetoric- Propaganda	Pop culture Elections

Perhaps you could inform others about a hobby. Maybe you have a personal interest in stages and theories of child development because you have a new niece or nephew. Or your major or current events offer a controversy that you can develop into a researched argument. Be sure the topic you choose can be narrowed to fit the assigned length of the paper as well as to fit an assigned purpose.

Once you have a general topic, whether chosen or assigned, you are ready to begin your focusing activities. Questions are among the best ways to focus. You can create your own questions specific to your topic(s) or try some of these. You might write down your responses, simply think about the questions, or discuss them with a friend, classmate, tutor, or teacher. Keep in mind that writing leaves you with a record of ideas for future drafting or to share with your teacher. Sometimes you cannot choose a topic and will need to show your instructor that you have been trying, and how you have approached the exploration of topics.

Freewrite for 5 minutes without regard for grammar, correctness, or audience.

- Why do I care about this topic?
- What do I know about my topic?
- What do I believe about my topic?

52

- What is a possible conflict?*
- What would I like to learn about my topic?
- Have I read anything recent about my topic?
- What questions would my reader have?
- Where can I find information on my topic?
- Does my school have a department or major in this topic area?
- Where might I find an expert on my topic?
- How does this topic affect my community?
- How does this topic impact me personally?

*useful for argumentative assignments

You may want to complete this exercise for more than one topic if you cannot choose yet. When you have found a topic(s), and written about that topic(s), and tried to focus, consider taking a break. Put the assignment and your prewriting aside and do something else. Depending upon your paper's due date, a brief walk in the fresh air may be all you can schedule. If you have more time, then take a full day. By putting the ideas aside, you come back refreshed and able to see the possibilities more clearly. (Caution: This part of the writing process is important; however, taking a break can easily become a procrastination technique. Guard against procrastination.)

You have thought, written, rested, and now it is time to make some decisions. You need to confirm your topic and consider possible approaches to that topic. At this time you are ready to create a tentative thesis. This is not the same as the thesis that will govern the paper. This tentative thesis is only a guiding idea that will allow you to structure your research. This is not a committed relationship. If a silly metaphor will work, consider your tentative thesis to be a blind date. Things might work out, you might suddenly get ill and need to leave, or you might even meet someone else. Regardless, you have begun your paper.

Finding Sources

Planning your research will save you time and result in more and better information. How much time will you allow for researching? Where will you do your research? What kinds of sources will you look for? What search terms will you use? Be prepared for each research session by writing a plan of what you will accomplish and how long you will take to accomplish it.

A good place to begin your research is with general sources like dictionaries, encyclopedias, general readership publications, and Internet searches. These resources will give you a background in your topic and offer feedback on the relative success of your search terms. You may even be fortunate in finding a bibliography or two in encyclopedia entries or Internet sites. Follow up on the leads these references offer.

You will certainly find some quality information online, but do not rely on the Web for all of your research, as there is a lot of trash out there. To begin evaluating the credibility of an Internet site, look at the domain of the URL (universal resource locator). This means the suffix of the Web address: **.gov**, **.edu**, **.org**, **.com**. Each kind of website has a some kind of bias or agenda. For example, www.loc.gov is a government site, the Library of Congress; www.oakland.edu is a state university in Michigan, Oakland University; www.soulofacitizen.org/ is a nonprofit site, a place to learn about community service and a book by Paul Rogat Loeb; and www.amazon.com is a commercial site, a place to engage in e-commerce. Consider the goals and objectives of each site you find, and analyze the site's use of rhetorical strategies. Is the site successful in accomplishing its purpose? What kinds of sites will offer the most suitable information for your paper?

After browsing the Internet and broad-readership publications, you need to pursue **articles in scholarly journals**. Generally, a scholarly journal is defined by these three characteristics: 1. a list of references at the end; 2. an author, his or her affiliation and credentials; and 3. no advertisements. Authoritative, well-researched information is present in articles from these academic journals, and you can find them in your campus library, electronic databases such as Research Navigator, and, occasionally, online. Your scholarly research, and even your Web browsing, will be most efficient at the library. All resources housed physically or electronically have been analyzed and evaluated by a professional librarian, which means the quality of the text has been determined for you. This means less time determining the reliability of sources and more efficient searches.

Government documents are materials produced by the United States Government Printing Office (GPO). Your campus library may be a full or partial government documents depository library, so you will have access to materials on topics as varied as "aluminum" and "zebras." Government websites are also available to you. Most research papers will benefit by including Census data; Congressional hearings, bills, or reports; or decisions handed down by the judiciary.

You should also take the time to browse through electronic databases such as Research Navigator, provided to you by Prentice Hall. Electronic databases include bibliographic files of articles (sometimes full text), reports, and occasionally, books that can be searched by author, title, or keywords. Be sure to provide as much information as possible in the search function, or you may wind up with thousands of "hits" that may not be directly related to your paper topic. Research Navigator is a particularly useful source due to the sheer volume of credible sources it provides. You will be able to search hundreds of thousands of pages of research materials from three large, world-class databases (The *New York Times* Search by Subject Archive, EBSCO'S ContentSelect Academic Journal Database, and "Best of the Web" Link Library) all in one place on the Internet. To access Research Navigator, visit www.researchnavigator.com and use the login/password provided on the inside-front cover of this book.

Finally, many instructors request or require **field research**. This means gathering your own evidence through an interview, survey, experiment, or observation. You will contribute to the scholarly dialog by adding new data, not just synthesizing existing data. Consider interviewing one or more authorities on your topic. Start early in order to schedule an interview that allows you to meet your writing deadlines. Prepare your questions in advance; dress professionally and be on time for your appointment; and send a thank you note after the interview. A survey is also a good way to gather data about trends and beliefs. Even running an experiment or attending an event will offer readers new information. See your instructor for assistance in designing and executing your fieldwork.

You will likely be surprised by some of what you find in your research, or at least you can hope you will. A research project that does not reveal new information becomes very boring. A research paper of any length will require you to read many more texts than you will include in the actual paper. Anything and everything you learn about your topic, even things you do not cite in the paper, will be indirectly present in your writing because of your confidence and competence. The more you know, the higher-level your thinking will be. Read. Take notes. Summarize. Read some more. Read until you are no longer surprised by what you find. The drafting and revising of your paper becomes much easier if you commit adequate time and care to the discovery of ideas.

Drafting Your Paper

The word *draft* can be used as a noun or a verb. As a noun, draft means the earliest version(s) of your paper: you have sentences and paragraphs. As a verb, draft means performing the actions, steps, or strategies a writer uses when creating a full version of his or her text. While you may draft at any point in the writing process, most drafting occurs after a writer has completed substantial research, reading, and prewriting.

Begin drafting someplace, any place (the middle, beginning, or end). The important thing is to put pen to paper, or fingers to keyboard, and write. Contrary to popular belief, if it's worth doing, it's worth doing badly several times. No one begins and ends with their first draft, not even the most gifted scholar and writer.

As you draft, give yourself permission to write badly. Your draft is an opportunity to explore structure and organization and figure out what you think about what you have learned. Try calling your first draft your "icky draft." Writer's block is not an issue if you just write. Write anything. Answer questions. Write in crayon. Write on a brown paper grocery bag. Choose the strategies that work best for you, but remain aware of other strategies, as you may need them at a different time or with a different assignment.

Strategies for Drafting

The following is a list of suggested strategies. Which ones might help you draft your paper?

- Be sure you are in a comfortable setting and have all of your supplies and research with you.
- Allow yourself to make mistakes.
- Carry blank pages with you wherever you go, so you can jot down a paragraph when it comes to you.
- Don't write yourself into a corner. Leave a place to begin—like half of a sentence for the next time you sit down to write.
- Draw a picture.
- Go on tangents. You never know where fabulous ideas may emerge.
- Write a letter or e-mail to a friend or someone else who would be interested in your topic. Talking to a specific audience in an informal note allows you to express yourself without thinking about what your teacher will think.
- Write a letter or e-mail to someone who is an authority on your topic. Send your letter.
- Start in the middle, as the introduction can be a hard place to start.
- Start with an introduction you know you will cut, just to get writing. Once you reach the conclusion, you can go back and completely rewrite the introduction to suit the paper you actually write.
- Write from a position that conflicts with your thesis.
- Allow yourself adequate time to consider the draft and think about where to go with your ideas. This means allow for breaks.
- Write/type several main points you want to cover, kind of an informal outline, and move around the document, jotting sentences under each heading as ideas come to you.
- Put aside everything you have written. Then write everything you can remember about your topic. This allows you to focus on what is most compelling. Sometimes a fresh start is easier than trying to fix a weak draft.

After a draft or two, your paper will have a shape, albeit an icky one in some cases. With your draft, you can move to detailed questions of tone, audience, specific purpose, and specific thesis.

You need to recognize the **tone** of your essay in order to control it. How would you describe the mood you wish to convey? Neutral? Frustrated? Pleased? How might your tone shift throughout the paper? What tone does your reader expect? The sample student paper by Alex Hollier at the end of this chapter provides a good example of the importance of tone. Throughout his research, Alex was turned off by the biased tone he found; in fact, the tone of many authors damaged or destroyed the validity and credibility of their work. Even when authors argued for his beliefs, Alex often found the overly passionate tone to be a problem. In his paper, he sought to present a neutral tone, and he was concerned this neutral tone might lead his readers to believe he did not care about the topic or paper. He monitored, discussed, and revised tone throughout the writing process.

Be familiar with your specific **audience** in order to anticipate questions, conflicts, and confusion. Who is your specific audience? In what magazine or journal might you publish your essay? What do they know about your topic? What are their beliefs about your topic? What reasons do they cite? What does demographic data reveal about your audience? Knowing this information allows you to choose appropriate levels of detail, diction, and style. If you audience does not know anything about violent behavior in relationship to playing violent video games, then you need to explain the issue.

You may have been assigned a general informative or argumentative **purpose**, but now it is time to get specific about the purpose of your paper. What do you wish to accomplish with this text? (And assume that passing the class is not what your instructor is looking for here.) Would you like to see a change in readers' actions? Do you seek a change in thought? Do you simply wish to call attention to an issue and leave the solutions to be discussed in other essays? What do you want readers to think, believe, change, or do after reading your paper?

Remember, all writing is of value, even if it seems unsuccessful. Each time you explore a piece of your writing, you learn something about language and your topic.

Developing a Thesis Statement

Along with the development of tone, audience, and purpose, you need to focus attention on your thesis; your guiding idea--tentative thesis--needs to become a concrete statement. Your thesis statement, which is a sentence or two placed early in your paper, must tell readers your topic and your position on your topic. Here are some examples:

1. Current welfare reform policy in the United States is not reducing the number of families living in poverty.
    (Topic: Welfare reform. Position: It is not reducing poverty.)

2. Research demonstrates that smaller public school classes will increase student learning.
    (Topic: Student learning. Position: Smaller classes will improve it.)

3. There are three learning styles—visual, auditory, and kinesthetic.
    (Topic: Learning styles. Position: There are three.)

You may also choose to include main points in your thesis. This works well in guiding readers through longer papers.

1. Current welfare reform policy in the United States is not reducing the number of families living in poverty because it does not adequately address problems of affordable housing, education and training, and employment opportunities.

2. Research demonstrates that smaller public school classes will increase student learning by increasing individual instruction, assessment, and feedback.

3. There are three learning styles—visual, auditory, and kinesthetic. Surveys and tests can identify the primary learning style of an individual.

The main points should be in the same order as they appear in the body of the paper.

Developing your thesis requires special attention to diction and order. You want the words to communicate your exact plan, and you want the structure to mirror the body of the text.

Synthesizing Information

Quality research and your own experiences and observations are necessary to a high quality research paper, but you need to step further into the intellectual process than simply juxtaposing secondary and personal data/ideas. You need to make connections, create insights that could not exist without your creative and critical thinking. A cliché works well here: You want your whole paper to be greater than the sum of its parts. This is an ambitious but achievable goal.

Take what you have learned from your research and look at it beside what you have experienced and observed in your own life. How do things connect? What contradictions are present? How can you reconcile contradictions? What common ground exists?

Using Sources in Your Paper

The purpose of using outside sources in your paper is to develop the content and credibility of your writing. You want the evidence you use to be reliable, verifiable, sufficient, and ethical. Ethical references do not take author(s) out of context, manipulate statistics, or otherwise present evidence in a manner not intended by the original author.

There are three main ways to incorporate secondary sources in your writing. Each type of evidence requires an in-text citation, which is explained in the **MLA Documentation** section.

Direct quotation is when you borrow exact words from a text and put those words in quotation marks. This is a good way add authority, content, and specific diction to your paper. When quoting, use only parts of sentences in order to communicate the essential meaning of the passage but to maintain the flow of your paper. Including too many long quotes makes the paper look like a patchwork quilt of other voices. Be sure your voice has primacy.

Paraphrase is putting short passages of a source into your own words. This is good way to weave ideas into your paper while maintaining your voice and flow. Be sure to use your own words and not the author's exact words.

Summary refers to using your own words to reduce a text to its essential ideas: thesis, main points, and conclusions. Summary presents a large body of information in a condensed form while maintaining your voice, tone, and flow.

MLA Documentation

The purpose of documenting sources is to give credit to others for their work, whether direct quote, paraphrase, summary, fact, visual, or other evidence. Proper MLA documentation in your research paper means you incorporate in-text citations (sometimes called parenthetical citations) and a works cited page (a list of all sources referenced in the paper). The information in the parenthesis tells readers exactly which author you are borrowing from. The works cited list then tells your reader the publication details of the source and how he or she can retrieve the same source.

Underlying the importance of correctness in documentation is the absolute necessity to **avoid plagiarism**. Plagiarism is the use of another's words or ideas without giving credit to the author. Incorrect and omitted documentation are plagiarism. Error in documentation, even if unintentional, may not seem as bad to you as deliberately cutting and pasting entire paragraphs or buying a paper, but error or malice in academic behavior are both problematic. Unintentional errors and oversights indicate that a student has not achieved mastery in the conventions of research writing; deliberate cheating and stealing indicate that a student has not accepted responsibility for his or her academic and ethical behavior. Regardless of form, plagiarism indicates a need for corrective action, either at the classroom or administrative level. Familiarize yourself with the academic conduct policy at your school.

Revising Your Paper

Revision is the art of rewriting or rethinking a piece of writing. Once you have a draft, a shape for your paper, you will want to address the quality of your presentation. You want to convey both your ideas and your credibility, so you need to revise for global—essay level—issues of unity, organization, transition, coherence, and flow. While these rhetorical issues can be addressed during drafting, most writers include them in the revision stage. **Unity**, which is desirable, is demonstrated when all main points, details, and evidence are directly connected to the thesis/claim. While creating a sense of **organization** is a large part of drafting, polishing that organization is important in the revision stage. Look for connections and natural **transitions** between and within your paragraphs.

Transitioning:	planned repetition of language;
	transitional words or expressions;
	parallelism;
	repeated image or idea;
	logical connection between two images or ideas;
	theme or symbol;
	summarize the preceding paragraph.

You may need to move paragraphs to improve the organization. **Internal transitions**, connections within paragraphs, should be clear to readers. To strengthen **coherence**, check the logic of sentence order and look for ways to use transitional words or phrases.

Since you want your paper to read smoothly and logically, you will have to carefully analyze your writing. What works? What doesn't work? What do you need to do to improve the quality of the text? Revision is your opportunity to make sure your paper communicates what you want to your audience.

Strategies for Revising:
- Read the paper to someone else. Note places where you stumble.
- Have someone else read the paper to you. Where does the text sound vague?
- Outline the paper, looking for gaps in information and research as well as organization.
- Seek feedback from others.
- Print the most recent version of the paper, cut the paragraphs apart, and move the pieces of paper around looking for patterns and possibilities, not just concerns.
- Get some distance; then look at your paper with "fresh eyes."

Editing Your Paper

Editing means taking time to address local—sentence level—issues such as correctness of punctuation and mechanics, diction, and sentence variety. Try editing backwards. To do this, isolate and check the last sentence, then the second to last sentence, then the third to last sentence. Doing this takes the ideas out of context, so you can focus on sentence structure. Do the backwards process at least three times. Each time, look for different issues. If you know you struggle with commas, look closely at commas. If you struggle with apostrophes, look closely at apostrophes. If you frequently use the wrong word, look closely at usage. Finally, edit for **wordiness,** which can be a problem for students trying to meet length requirements. Add more ideas and support for your thesis/claim. Cut all unnecessary or repeated words and ideas.

Spend some time focusing on, even pondering, **diction**—language usage—during your editing. Be aware of denotative (dictionary) and connotative (implied or associated) meanings, so each word does its job and no word is distracting to readers. An additional consideration when choosing or polishing diction is analyzing the sound and tone of each word. Does the word have hard sounds? soft sounds? Which kind of sound fits the sentence and paragraph best?

Combine sentence structures using subordination and coordination to show relationships between ideas. Deliberate attention to sentence patterns can improve rhythm, flow, and readability. However, the primary job of **sentence variety** is to demonstrate relationships between ideas. Consider using compound sentences, which show equal relationships between two or more ideas; complex sentences, which show unequal relationships between two or more ideas; and compound-complex sentences, which show complicated relationships between several ideas. Even though simple sentences work to create emphasis and state facts clearly, too many simple sentences can become boring, so be sure to consider the overall balance of your sentences.

Conclusion

Ultimately, whatever steps you take when writing—for there is not a single process—your goal is to hand in research papers with confidence, which necessitates successful selection and application of rhetorical strategies.

Alex Hollier

Professor Smith

Rhetoric 160, Section 003

December 10, 20xx

To Take Arms Against a Sea of Troubles

The first ten amendments to the U.S. Constitution, collectively known as the Bill of Rights, enumerate certain rights possessed by American citizens. However, in our modern society, many of the rights we enjoy have taken on an added dimension of responsibility. For example, the First Amendment guarantees the right to free speech. It may be argued, though, that the right to free speech also carries with it the responsibility to exercise that right as circumstances may require. I believe that the Second Amendment also falls under the category of a right with responsibility. The American people should exercise their Second Amendment right to bear arms because it would aid in the common defense of the nation, promote a higher degree of politeness, and give citizens a greater degree of safety and security in their homes.

An armed populace deters any potential aggressor from launching an invasion of our country and acts as a safeguard against a tyrannical government. It is so effective in this latter role that many repressive governments disarm their people as one of their first acts after achieving power. In order to improve the defense and security of the nation, I propose that the American people take up arms and become proficient in their use.

The right to bear arms was explicitly spelled out in the Constitution by the founders at the birth of our nation. The Second Amendment to the

Constitution clearly states, "A well regulated militia, being necessary to the security of a free state, the right of the people to keep and bear arms, shall not be infringed" (United States). The first rationale for this had just been graphically demonstrated in the Revolutionary War. During this war, the Continental Army was largely comprised of ordinary citizens, many with little or no formal military training. Additionally, the colonial militias provided many additional soldiers. Most of the militias did not even wear the most rudimentary of uniforms. The only equipment that these volunteers had was their personal firearms, most of which they brought with them from home. This ragtag force fought and eventually defeated the professional soldiers of the English army, which was comprised largely of veteran soldiers with significant combat experience in previous military campaigns. The English army was widely considered to be the most powerful fighting force in the world at the time. Among the factors that led to the American victory were the ready availability of firearms among the populace (especially critical once the naval blockades prevented the acquisition of additional guns) and the easy familiarity that the average colonist had with the weapons of the day. At the time of the Revolution, almost every household possessed at least one gun. These were important tools in a time when a significant portion of the family's diet was obtained through hunting. Also, it was considered traditional for a father to teach the basics of firearm usage to his young sons, so that they could assist in the hunting chores. This tradition survives to this day, although it is not quite as widespread as it once was. Today, with our domestic security threatened as never before, the need for the public to be able to defend itself has never been greater.

The Constitution is readily accepted by readers as an authoritative source. Here Alex explains the context of the 2nd Amend. and why he interprets it as he does.

The second rationale for the Second Amendment had to do with the nation's defense against a more domestic form of aggression. At the time the Constitution was written, our nation had just fought a war of liberation against an unjust and repressive dictatorship. When setting up the government for the newly formed United States, the founders included many safeguards against a possible return of that kind of rule. Among these safeguards was the right of the populace to retain weaponry, instead of concentrating all of the nation's firepower in the hands of the government. This was viewed as the last resort, should the need arise, that a nation would have against its own government. The Declaration of Independence outlines the philosophical basis for the use of such force. It states that governments

Direct quotes are cited by author and page. The parenthetical statement includes parenthesis last name page number parenthesis period. No commas inside the parenthesis.

are instituted to preserve the rights of citizens, and that, ". . . whenever any form of government becomes destructive of these ends, it is the right of the people to alter or to abolish it, and to institute new government, laying its foundation on such principles..."(Risjord 451). The right of the people to bear arms provides the means for the right to alter the government, should all other means fail. Many of the founders were in favor of the occasional rebellion in the name of liberty. Thomas Jefferson, in a letter to James

Jefferson's quote is taken from the Bartlett and Kaplan text. (qtd, in Bartlett and Kaplan 343) tells readers this is an indirect quote.

Madison, wrote that, "a little rebellion, now and then, is a good thing, and as necessary in the political world as storms in the physical" (qtd. in Bartlett and Kaplan 343). This safeguard of an armed nation has been a remarkably successful one as the United States has maintained democratic rule for over two hundred years.

This paragraph presents four examples from world history which explain why the populace should not be disarmed.

Historically, among the first acts of any totalitarian regime is to disarm the public. Following the Russian Revolution in 1917, one of Lenin's first decrees criminalized the private ownership of firearms. The

Examples
1. Russia
2. China
3. Britain-Scots
4. Britain-India

The use of historical comparisons adds both support for the thesis and support for the author's ethos (credibility and integrity).

The authority of Gandhi as a peace lover leads to the assumption that he would oppose an armed populace. This quote contradicts that assumption and leaves readers open to the claim in the following paragraph.

Main point #2:

Communists in China followed that example, as well, after they seized power. Both of these governments are (or were) considered to be among the most repressive of personal freedom. It is interesting to note that in the latter days of the Soviet government, the criminal syndicates in the major towns became extremely well armed, while the average law-abiding citizen was forbidden from owning even the simplest of firearms. The disarming of a subject populace was also accomplished to great effect by England against the Scots in the fourteenth century, and later by the British government against India in the twentieth. In both instances, the goal was to pacify a population and make them easier to conquer and rule. The Scots eventually won their freedom by a combination of concerted military action and irregular partisan conflict in a struggle that both philosophically and historically presaged the American Revolution. The Indian movement for independence was unique in history, depending as it did on a passive and peaceful resistance. However, even such a noted pacifist as Mahatma Gandhi was moved to state that, "Among the many misdeeds of the British rule in India, history will look upon the Act depriving a whole nation of arms as the blackest"(Quoteland).

As a citizen of the United States of America, I can only see having an armed populace as a positive virtue. Although many people think that guns are evil and have no place in civilized society, the civilized society that they speak of was fought for and won by peaceful people doing violence with guns. Without such people, the whole of civilization would have long ago fallen to the barbarians.

A well-armed society is inherently a safer and more polite one. The politeness comes from the fact that your fellow citizen is also armed and has

The ability to make his offense known. The increased safety comes from not

only the actual possession of the gun, but also the deterrent effect that any

one at any time might be armed.

For example, I point to the dueling code of France in the 17th

century. If a gentleman of this era was offended by the actions or words of

another, he could simply throw down a glove and present two options. The

offending party could apologize sincerely and think more carefully about his

behavior in the future, or he could pick up the glove and accept a duel. The

prospect of having to defend one's actions with one's life led to a more

careful consideration of the finer points of etiquette and politeness and to a

more frequent consideration of the viewpoints of others. The same could

apply in this country today. A modern interpretation of this concept might

be found in the works of Robert Heinlein. Heinlein, a Hugo Award-winning

author and noted futurist, often used his novels to confront societal issues. In

<u>Beyond this Horizon</u>, Heinlein describes a society in the not-too-distant

future where all citizens carry sidearms and would challenge each other to

duels. In this society, street crime and bloody brawls were mostly

nonexistent.

Over the last thirty years, many laws have been instituted to keep

firearms from falling into the so-called "wrong hands." One of the most

successful laws has been the Brady Bill, a law stating that any person who

wishes to purchase a handgun must wait five days for a background check

(to make sure that an applicant is legally allowed to own a hand gun). The

other rationale for this law is to keep guns out of the hands of angry,

impulsive people who try to buy a gun on the spur of the moment and use it

to hurt people (themselves or others) before they have a chance to relax and rationally consider the situation. This law was a brilliant idea and has improved public safety in this country without hampering the rights of citizens to be armed.

Acknowledgement of some assumptions about gun ownership. A rebuttal to these assumptions. And establishment of common ground with reader.

One effect of this law has been to virtually eliminate the market for a particularly dangerous type of handgun. Since the passage of the Brady Bill, the so-called "Saturday Night Special" has largely been abandoned by both gun manufacturers and gun buyers. These guns were cheap, unreliable, and appealed largely to criminals. Most of these guns were sold to people who knew nothing about guns or gun safety and were just as likely to harm an innocent bystander as their intended target. The departure of this class of handgun has been unmourned by serious gun collectors and enthusiasts. This law has helped to restrict gun ownership to those who are serious about it and who can accept the responsibilities that accompany the exercise of their Second Amendment right.

Many people believe that higher levels of gun ownership must inevitably lead to higher rates of gun violence. This is not necessarily the

The author and his credentials are in a signal phrase, so the parenthetical statement includes just the page number.

case. In an article published in The Canadian Review of Sociology and Anthropology, Marc Ouimet wrote that "[a]djoining U.S. states and Canadian provinces have similar rates of criminal homicide. This is a surprising result given the fact that firearm ownership is much more

comparison

prevalent in the northern U.S." (357). This supports the idea that the key to controlling gun violence is not the elimination of guns but the rational and effective regulation of their sale and use. The Smith & Wesson Corporation

An answer to criticism of the firearms industry.

has been the object of some criticism in the last few years because of a new policy of theirs. Before the sale of any of their firearms they will fire a round through it. By itself, this procedure is simply another test for quality control of the product. However, the company then retains the test bullet in storage. Herein lies the controversy. When a bullet is fired through a gun, the rifling in the barrel leaves a distinct pattern on the bullet. As a fingerprint can be used to identify a specific person, the rifling pattern can be used to identify the specific gun that fired a given bullet. Many civil libertarians are afraid of the potential implications for abuse of this information. However, law-abiding citizens should not be concerned by this.

The author distinguishes his claim from similar positions. He argues for access to firearms for law-abiding citizens and a system to "monitor" fire arms for law enforcement officials. Alex goes even further in stating his desire that corporations would follow the lead of Smith and Wesson; thus, the need for state controlled gun registries would be eliminated.

The only reason that an individual might face scrutiny through this is if his or her guns were used in the commission of a crime. This policy simply removes the anonymity from gunfire by allowing bullets to be traced back to the owner of the gun that fired them. I support this idea one hundred percent. It would eliminate the need for the long and costly hours that the police spend every year futilely searching for ballistic matches when the database they have to work with is incomplete at best. If more gun companies would adopt this policy it would replace the inadequate gun registrations that most states use.

Claim of policy.

John Lott Jr., a senior research scholar at Yale Law School and the author of <u>More Guns, Less Crime</u>, pointed out how the current laws are largely useless in his article published in the <u>National Review</u>. Lott states that gun licensing is only effective if the criminal leaves the gun at the scene of the crime and he or she took the time to register the gun in the first place (30).

In our society, if a citizen sees an unlawful act being committed, his or her only option is to call the police and wait for them to come and take care of the problem. This is not a major threat to society with respect to crimes such as shoplifting, illegal parking, or tax fraud. However, in

Cautious use of narrative and pathos (appeal to emotions).

situations where people's lives are in imminent danger, this lag time in police response may prove fatal. Such is the case of the Luby's Cafeteria massacre in Killeen, Texas, in 1991. On October 16, twenty-four people were killed and twenty others were injured. Gratia Hupp, a patron of the restaurant, had to watch the deaths of both of her parents at the hands of a madman while she was unable to do anything about it. Hupp later stated that she could have prevented that tragedy if she had only been allowed to carry a firearm. She went on to become a proponent of the "shall issue" form of

Parenthetical citation tells readers this narrative is on page 164 of Josh Sugarman's, Every Handgun is Aimed at You.

concealed carry laws (Sugarmann 164). The "shall issue" type of law obligates the local government to issue a concealed carry permit to any applicant who meets its criteria rather than placing the onus on the applicants to prove their need for such a permit. Nelson Lund, a professor of law at George Mason University, goes as far as to say "each permit creates a deterrent effect that saves society something like $ 3,000-$ 5,000, plus any unmeasured benefits such as a greater sense of safety and peacefulness" (35).

The reason that these types of violent outbursts still happen is because the perpetrators have little to fear. The average citizen is not armed, and most criminals know this. If we as law-abiding citizens make a stand

A call to action for all law-abiding citizens.

and show criminals that we will no longer be victimized but instead fight back, then criminals will have only two options: take up another line of work, or face an equally armed adversary. I believe that most will do the former, as most criminals are inherent cowards who prey on the weak and live in fear of the day when no one fears them.

Summary of main point #2.

An armed society, then, offers many advantages to its citizenry. It offers them substantial incentive to be polite as well as the enjoyment of such politeness. It also offers the security of physical safety. These advantages also come with a price to be paid in the form of increased regulation and responsibility. However, this is a small price to pay for these benefits.

Main point #3:
On the Home Front

It seems that in this modern age in which we live very few citizens live in a town where "you can leave your doors unlocked." However, it seems that most of us are under the impression that a dead bolt lock is all that we need to protect ourselves from home invasion. This a common misconception, largely promulgated by manufacturers of locks. In most instances, such passive means as locked doors are sufficient to keep us safe in our homes. However, in emergencies, more active steps must be taken to keep our families and ourselves safe. Guns provide the means for such an active defense.

This paragraph
seeks to establish
that the use of guns
for home safety is a
cultural tradition

We, the people, need to be able to defend our homes and families. Since before the founding of this country, Americans have kept weapons in their homes as a means of protection. In the modern age, of course, the threats of marauding Indian tribes and cattle rustlers are greatly diminished. Today's threats are the thieves and lunatics whose actions fill the headlines of the local papers and occasionally break into the nightly news. As long as honest people work to accumulate wealth and as long as dishonest people seek to appropriate that wealth, the threat of robbery will always be with us. Lt. Col. Timothy A. Capron, PhD., commander of the Nuclear Weapons Training Detachment at the Nuclear Weapons School in Kirtland, New

Statistical evidence
makes crime in the
home a reality.

Mexico, estimates in 1992 that "24 percent of the nation's households were touched by crime last year" (113). Keep in mind that this is not one quarter of the homes of China, Russia, Australia or any other country on the other side of the world, but one out of four homes in the communities in

An appeal to readers' sense of belongingness.

which we live. This is happening to our fellow citizens, our friends, our neighbors, and our families.

While our police and sheriffs do all that they can to protect the inhabitants of their towns, they cannot always respond in time to prevent harm to innocents. Police response time, especially in rural areas, is often not sufficient to protect citizens from criminals who strike without warning. Citizens, in this circumstance, have no other choice but to depend on

Signal phrase is used to introduce a direct quote and statistics.

themselves for protection. In an article published in The Journal of Criminal Law and Criminology titled "Armed Resistance to Crime: The Prevalence and Nature of Self-Defense with a Gun," authors Gary Kleck and Marc Gertz draw an interesting comparison between criminals and law-abiding gun owners. They estimate that "while 1.1 million violent crimes are committed annually with guns, approximately 2.5 million citizens employ guns each year to defend themselves from criminals" (155). Some communities in the world have taken to using their citizens as an active police force. Dr. Ray Abrahams, a lecturer in social anthropology at Cambridge University, wrote about an instance of this in his book Vigilant Citizens. In the Tanzanian village of Busangi, all men, young or old, must carry a bow, arrows, and a whistle at all times. If a crime is committed, all the men of the village are to act as their own police force and track the perpetrators down, using the whistles as a means of communication. This policy was so successful that many villages in the surrounding area adopted it as well (27).

What are law-abiding citizens supposed to do if someone breaks into their homes? Should they calmly say, "Please, take everything I own, and don't forget to kill us before you leave"? Should they just call the police, hide like cowards, and hope the intruder doesn't find their families or themselves before help can arrive? How could parents teach their children to walk with their heads held high if this is the example that has been set for them?

This paragraph presents data supporting gun ownership as a deterrent to criminals.

Also, the possibility that the residents of a dwelling may be armed must surely be a deterrent to any potential intruder who may contemplate such a crime. In an article for Social Forces titled "Gun Availability and Violent Crime: New Evidence from the National Incident-Based Reporting System," Lisa Stolzenberg and Stewart J. D'Alessio refer to a survey of 1,900 incarcerated felons. In this study, "three-fifths of the surveyed felons acknowledged that they were more fearful of confronting an armed victim than a law enforcement officer" (1470). Also, "40% of the felons reported that they decided not to commit a crime because they thought that the intended victim might be armed" (1470). Today, with rates of gun ownership relatively low, a criminal may break into a home with little fear of meeting an armed response from the homeowner. As the rates of gun ownership increase in an area with a correspondingly greater chance for an intruder to get shot, the number of robbers and robberies will go down – one way or another.

Fear for the safety of children is addressed.

There are those who feel that a gun in the house makes it less safe, rather than safer. This is due to the potential for accidents caused by children or others who are unaware of gun safety. The correct response to such ignorance is education. Children should be taught gun safety, and all adults should be proficient in the operation of firearms.

In a study titled, "Seeing Is Believing: What Do Boys Do When They Find a Real Gun?" published by The American Academy of Pediatrics, Geoffrey A. Jackman, Mirna M. Farah, Arthur L. Kellermann, and Harold K. Simon found some interesting results when they placed small groups of children in a room with a specially designed gun in a drawer. The gun was designed to look and feel like a real gun but was harmless and sent a signal to a computer every time the trigger was pulled. Their research found that of the sixty-four boys in the study, forty-eight found the gun; one left the room to tell an adult; thirty handled it; thirty-two thought it was a toy; sixteen pulled the trigger; and one boy disassembled it and put it back together again (1247). This study was excellent to help convince parents that they should be safe in their handling of firearms around children. Also, it points out the need for parents to educate their children about gun safety – whether or not they keep guns in their own house. However, the original study was limited in its scope. An interesting follow-up to this study would have been to educate the participating children in a formal gun safety class. The test could then be repeated to gauge the effectiveness of gun safety programs in altering real-world behavior.

Many things in the home have the potential to cause injury. These include electrical outlets, hot stove burners, and stairs. I do not think any reasonable person would respond to the many injuries caused each year by these items by banning them. While living in the dark and eating cold food in one-story buildings may hold some attraction for a few, I do not think such an extreme solution is necessary for our nation as a whole. Dave Kopel does a good job of disarming some of the most popular antigun contentions in his article, "An Army of Gun Lies." For example, a figure often spouted is that "…owning a gun is associated with a 2.7 times greater risk of being murdered" (30). This figure is based on a rather serious methodological error. Those that use this statement are mistaking cause for effect. High crime rates raise the fear of being victimized by crime. This fear leads to a greater rate of gun ownership. High crime rates are the cause of high rates of gun ownership, not the effect. The study also showed that owning a security system increases risk by about the same factor, due to the same reasons, yet no one can seriously argue that security systems are a causative factor in crime (30).

Instead of questioning the claim in line 3, Alex invalidates the statistic by pointing to flaws in the methods used to determine the statistic.

In summation, arming the populace as a whole will aid in the common defense of the nation, promote a higher degree of politeness, and give citizens a greater degree of safety and security in their homes. I do not claim that this idea will create a utopian society. It will not do away with the national debt, save the rain forests, or eliminate anthrax. However, it will, I believe, create a better society. Many nations have attempted to enact universal disarmament of their citizenry. That solution has not been met with any notable degree of success. On the other hand, arming the nation as whole has never been tried in the modern age. It may just be the next step in the evolution of civilized society.

Transitional phrase is used to signal the conclusion. As with many extended arguments, this essay closes with a summary of the main points and goals of the paper .

Works Cited

Abrahams, Ray. <u>Vigilant Citizens</u>. Malden, MA: Polity Press, 1998.

Bartlett, John and Justin Kaplan, eds. <u>Bartlett's Familiar Quotations</u>.

Boston: Little, Brown and Company, 1992.

Capron, Timothy A. "What's the Real Story on Crime Statistics?" <u>Security</u>

<u>Management</u>. 36.8 (1992): 113,114.

Heinlein, Robert A. <u>Beyond This Horizon</u>. New York: Penguin Books,

1997.

Jackman, Geoffrey, Mirna M. Farah, Arthur L. Kellermann, and Harold K.

Simon. "Seeing Is Believing: What Do Boys Do When They Find a

Real Gun?" <u>Pediatrics</u>. 107.6 (2001): 1247.

Kleck, Gary, and Marc Gertz. "Armed Resistance to Crime: The Prevalence

and Nature of Self-Defense with a Gun." <u>Journal of Criminal Law</u>

<u>and Criminology</u>. 86 (1995): 150-87.

Kopel, Dave. "An Army of Gun Lies." <u>National Review</u> 52.7 (2000):

28-35.

Lott, John R. Jr. "When Gun Control Costs Lives." <u>National Forum</u>. 80.4

(2000): 29-32.

Lund, Nelson. "Gunning Down Crime; The Statistics of Concealed

Weapons." <u>The Weekly Standard</u>. (1998): 35.

Ouimet, Marc. "Crime in Canada and in the United States: A Comparative

Analysis." <u>The Canadian Review of Sociology and Anthropology</u>.

36.3 (1999): 329-408. 10 March 2003

<www.researchnavigator.com>

The citations are in alphabetical order.

The use of a hanging indentation tells readers that the citation is not complete.

Multiple authors of an article in a journal.

Alex uses a variety of current scholarly books and journal articles as well as web resources and general readership publications.

Quoteland. Home Page. 31 Oct. 2001.

<http://www.quoteland.com/qldb/author/303>

Risjord, Norman K. America, a History of the United States. Engelwood

Cliffs, New Jersey: Prentice Hall, 1988.

Stolzenberg, Lisa, and Stewart J. D'Alessio. "Gun Availability and Violent

Crime: New Evidence from the National Incident-Based Reporting

System." Social Forces. 78.4 (2000): 1461-82. 10 March 2003

<www.researchnavigator.com>

Sugarmann, Josh. Every Handgun is Aimed at You. New York: The New

Press, 2001.

United States. Bill of Rights. Washinton: GPO, 1791. 10 March 2003

<www.researchnavigator.com>

*Article from
Research Navigator.*

*Research Navigator
allows Alex to
retrieve government
and legal
documents.*

Appendix A

Documenting Your Electronic Sources

Copyright laws came into effect when people started realizing that income could be made by selling their words. In an era dubbed "The Age of Information," knowledge and words are taking on more significance than ever. Laws requiring writers to document or give credit to the sources of their information, while evolving, are still in effect.

Various organizations have developed style manuals detailing, among other style matters, how to document sources in their particular disciplines. For writing in English composition and literature, Modern Language Association (MLA) and American Psychological Association (APA) guidelines are the most commonly used, but others, such as those in *The Chicago Manual of Style* (CMS), are available. Always find out from your instructor what style to use in a specific assignment so that you can follow the appropriate guidelines.

For general information on MLA and APA citations, the best print sources are:

> Gibaldi, Joseph. MLA Handbook for Writers of Research Papers. 5th ed. NY: MLA, 1999.

> American Psychological Association. (2001). *Publication Manual of the American Psychological Association* (5th ed.). Washington: APA.

Because the methods of obtaining electronic information are developing so rapidly, printed style manuals have had difficulty in keeping up with the changes and in developing documentation styles for electronic sources. As a result, the most up-to-date information from the MLA and the APA about documenting online sources with URLs can be found on these organizations' websites. This Appendix shows you how to credit your electronic sources based on the information there.

When you cite electronic sources, it is vital to type every letter, number, symbol, and space accurately. Any error makes it impossible to retrieve your source. Since electronic sources tend to be transitory, printing a hard copy of your sources will make it easier for you to cite accurately and provide evidence for your documentation. MLA style encloses Internet addresses and URLs (Uniform Resource Locators) in angle brackets < >. If you see them around an address, do not use them as part of the address when you attempt to retrieve the source. APA style does not enclose URLs.

Modern Language Association (MLA) Style Guidelines

These guidelines follow the documentation style authorized by the Modern Language Association for electronic sources. Web sources are documented in basically the same way as traditional sources. According to the MLA website, the following items should be included if they are available:

1. Name of the author, editor, compiler, or translator of the source (if available and relevant), reversed for alphabetizing and followed by an abbreviation, such as ed., if appropriate
2. Title of a poem, short story, article, or similar short work within a scholarly project, database, or periodical (in quotation marks); or title of a posting to a discussion list or forum (taken from the subject line and put in quotation marks), followed by the description Online posting
3. Title of a book (underlined)
4. Name of the editor, compiler, or translator of the text (if relevant and if not cited earlier), preceded by the appropriate abbreviation, such as ed.
5. Publication information for any print version of the source
6. Title of the scholarly project, database, periodical, or professional or personal site (underlined); or, for a professional or personal site with no title, a description such as Homepage
7. Name of the editor of the scholarly project or database (if available)
8. Version number of the source (if not part of the title) or, for a journal, the volume number, issue number, or other identifying number
9. Date of electronic publication, of the latest update, or of posting
10. For a posting to a discussion list or forum, the name of the list or forum
11. The number range or total number of pages, paragraphs, or other sections, if they are numbered
12. Name of any institution or organization sponsoring or associated with the website
13. Date when the researcher accessed the source
14. Electronic address, or URL, of the source (in angle brackets)

Examples:

Book
Shaw, Bernard. <u>Pygmalion</u>. 1912. Bartleby Archive. 6 Mar. 1998 <http://www.columbia.edu/acis/ bartleby/shaw/>.

Poem
Carroll, Lewis. "Jabberwocky." 1872. 6 Mar. 1998.
    <http://www.jabberwocky.com/carroll/jabber/
    jabberwocky.html>.

Article in a Journal
Rehberger, Dean. "The Censoring of Project #17:
    Hypertext Bodies and Censorship." Kairos 2.2
    (Fall 1997): 14 secs. 6 Mar. 1998 <http://
    english.ttu.edu/kairos/2.2/index_f.html>.

Article in a Magazine
Viagas, Robert, and David Lefkowitz. "Capeman Closing
    Mar. 28." Playbill 5 Mar. 1998. 6 Mar. 1998
    <http://www1.playbill.com/cgi-bin/plb/news?cmd
    =show&code=30763>.

Article in a Newspaper
Sandomir, Richard. "Yankees Talk Trades in Broadcast
    Booth." New York Times on the Web 4 Dec. 2001. 5
    Dec. 2001 <http://www.nytimes.com/pages/
    business/media/index.html>.

Article in a Reference Database
"Jupiter." Britannica Online. Vers. 97.1.1 Mar. 1997.
    Encyclopaedia Britannica. 29 Mar. 1998 <http://
    www.eb.com:180>.

Posting to a Discussion List
Grumman, Bob. "Shakespeare's Literacy." Online
    posting. 6 Mar. 1998. Deja News. <humanities.
    lit.author>.

Scholarly Project
Voice of the Shuttle: Web Page for Humanities
    Research. Ed. Alan Liu. Mar. 1998. U of
    California Santa Barbara. 8 Mar. 1998
    <http://humanitas.ucsb.edu/>.

Professional Site
The Nobel Foundation Official Website. The Nobel
    Foundation. 28 Feb. 1998 <http://www.nobel.se/>.

Personal Site
Thiroux, Emily. Home page. 7 Mar. 1998
    <http://academic.csubak.edu/home/acadpro/
    departments/english/engthrx.htmlx>.

Government or Institutional Site
Zebra Mussels in Vermont. Homepage. State of Vermont
Agency of Natural Resources. 3 May 1998 <http://
www.anr.state.vt.us/dec/waterq/smcap.htm>.

Synchronous Communications (such as MOOs, MUDs, and IRCs)
Ghostly Presence. Group Discussion. telnet 16 Mar.
1997 <moo.du.org:8000/80anon/anonview/1
4036#focus>.

Gopher Sites
Banks, Vickie, and Joe Byers. "EDTECH." 18 Mar. 1997
<gopher://ericyr.syr.edu:70/00/Listservs/EDTECH/
README>.

FTP (File Transfer Protocol) Sites
U.S. Supreme Court directory. 6 Mar. 1998
<ftp://ftp.cwru.edu/U.S.Supreme.Court/>.

Online Work of Art
Van Gogh, Vincent. The Olive Trees. 1889. Museum of
Modern Art, New York. 5 Dec. 2001 <http://
www.moma.org/docs/collection/paintsculpt/
recent/c463.htm>.

Online Interview
Plaxco, Jim. Interview. Planetary Studies Foundation.
Oct. 1992. 5 Dec. 2001 <http://www.planets.org>.

Online Film or Film Clip
Columbus, Chris, dir. Harry Potter and the Sorcerer's
Stone. Trailer. Warner Brothers, 2001. 5 Dec.
2001 <http://hollywood.com>.

Electronic Television or Radio Program
Chayes, Sarah. "Concorde." All Things Considered.
Natl. Public Radio. 26 July 2000. 7 Dec. 2001
<http://www.npr.com/programs/atc/archives>.

Synchronous Communication
Author's last name, First name. Identifying label.
"Title of work." xx Month 20xx. Name of forum.
xx Month 20xx. <Telnet://lingua.networkname>.

Generally follow the guidelines for other online citations, modifying them
wherever necessary, but always provide as much information as possible. Some
cited material will require identifying labels (e.g., Interview or Online posting),
but such labels should be neither underlined nor set within quotation marks.
When documenting synchronous communications that are posted in MOO
(multiuser domain, object oriented) and MUD (multiuser domain) forums, name

the speaker or speakers; describe the event; provide the date of the event and the name of the forum (e.g., linguaMOO); and cite the date of access as well as the network name (including the prefix <u>Telnet://</u>).

Work from an Online Service

```
Author's last name, First name. Publication. 20xx.
     Internet Provider name. xx Month 20xx. Keyword:
     Name.
```
Or
```
Last name, First name. Publication. 20xx. Internet
     Provider name. xx Month 20xx. Path: Name; Name;
     Name.
```

```
Brash, Stephen B. "Bioprospecting the Public Domain."
     Cultural Anthropology 14.4 (1999): 535-56.
     ProQuest Direct. Teaneck Public Library,
     Teaneck, NJ. 7 Dec. 1999 <http://proquest.
     umi.com>.
```
Or
```
Dutton, Gail. "Greener Pigs." Popular Science 255.5
     (1999): 38-39. ProQuest Direct. Teaneck Public
     Library, Teaneck, NJ. 7 Dec. 1999 <http://
     proquest.umi.com>.
```

For works that have been accessed through an online service, either through a library service (e.g., ProQuest Direct or Lexis-Nexis) or through one of the large Internet providers (e.g., America Online), you may not know the URL of the source. In such cases, cite the keyword or path that led to the source, if applicable, and separate each individual item in the path with a semicolon; the keyword or path will be the last item in the citation. For sources accessed through library services, as above, cite the name of the service, the name of the library, the date you assessed the material, and the URL of the service's homepage. If you also know the name of the database used, include that information (underlined) before the name of the online service.

American Psychological Association (APA) Style Guidelines

The most recent (5th) edition of the *Publication Manual of the American Psychological Association* includes general guidelines for citing electronic sources, and the APA has published specific examples for documenting Web sources on its Web page. Go to:

<u>http://www.apastyle.org/elecre.html</u>

In general, document these sources as you do traditional sources, giving credit to the author and including the title and date of publication. Include as much information as possible to help your reader to be able to retrieve the information. Any sources that are not generally available to your readers should be documented within the body of your writing as a personal communication but not included in your reference list. Such sources include material from listservs, newsgroups, Internet relay chats (IRCs), MOOs, MUDs, and e-mail.

According to information at the website for the American Psychological Association entitled "How to Cite Information From the World Wide Web," all references begin with the same information that would be provided for a printed source (or as much of that information as possible). The Web information is then placed at the end of the reference. It is important to use the "Retrieved from" and the date because documents on the Web may change in content, move, or be removed from a site altogether. To cite a website in text (but not a specific document), it's sufficient to give the address (e.g., http://www.apa.org) there. No reference entry is needed.

Use the following guidelines to include a source in your reference list:

```
Name of author [if given]. (Publication date) [in
     parentheses]. Title of the article [following
     APA guidelines for capitalization]. Title of
     periodical or electronic text [italicized].
     Volume number and/or pages [if any]. Retrieved
     [include the date here] from the World Wide Web:
     [include the URL here, and do not end with a
     period]
```

Examples:

Journal Article
```
Fine, M. A. & Kurdek, L. A. (1993, November).
     Reflections on determining authorship credit and
     authorship order on faculty-student
     collaborations. American Psychologist, 48.11,
     1141-1147. Retrieved March 6, 1998 from the
     World Wide Web: http://www.apa.org/journals/
     amp/kurdek.html
```

Newspaper Article
```
Murray, B. (1998, February). Email bonding with your
     students. APA Monitor [Newspaper, selected
     stories online]. Retrieved March 6, 1998 from
     the World Wide Web: http://www.apa.org/monitor/
     bond.html
```

World Wide Web Site

Williams, Scott. (1996, June 14). Back to school with the quilt. *AIDS Memorial Quilt Website.* Retrieved June 14, 1996, from http://www.aidsquilt.org/newsletter/stoires/backto.html

File Transfer Protocol (FTP), Telnet, or Gopher Site

Altar, T.W. (1993). *Vitamin B12 and vegans.* Retrieved May 28, 1996, from ftp://ftp.cs.yle.edu

King, Jr., M.L. (1963, August 28). I have a dream [speech]. Retrieved January 2, 1996, from telnet://ukanaix.cc.ukans.edu

Synchronous Communications (MOO, MUD, IRC)

Harnack, A. (1996, April 4). Words [Group discussion]. Retrieved April 5, 1996, from telnet://moo.du.org/port=8888

Web Discussion Forum

Holden, J.B. (2001, January 2). The failure of higher education [Formal discussion initiation]. Message posted to http://ifets.mtu.edu/archives

Listserv (electronic mailing list)

Weston, Heather (2002, June 12). Re: Registration schedule now available. Message posted to the Chamberlain Kronsage dormitory electronic mailing list, archived at http://listserv.registrar.uwsp.edu/archives/62.html

Newsgroup

Hotgirl (2002, January 12). Dowsing effort fails. Message posted to news://alt.science.esp3/html

Appendix B

Glossary

Boolean Comes from the ideas of British mathematician George Boole (1815-1964). From his writings come the Boolean operators: AND, OR, and NOT, used to link words and phrases for more precise queries for search engines and directories.

Database A repository of information that is searchable.

Domain One of the different subsets of the Internet. The suffix found on the host name of an Internet server defines its domain. For example, the host name for Prentice Hall, the publisher of this book, is www.prenhall.com. The last part, .COM, indicates that Prentice Hall is a part of the commercial domain. Other domains include .MIL for military, .EDU for education, .ORG for non-profit organizations, .GOV for government organizations, and many more.

Download The process of transferring a file, document, or program from a remote computer to a local computer. (See Upload.)

E-mail The short name for electronic mail. E-mail is sent electronically from one person to another. Some companies have e-mail systems that are not part of the Internet. E-mail can be sent to one person or to many different people.

Homepage In its specific sense, this refers to a Web document that a browser loads as its central navigational point to browse the Internet. It may also be used to refer to as a Web page describing an individual. In the most general sense, it is used to refer to any Web document.

Host Another name for a server computer. (See Server.)

HTML This is an abbreviation for HyperText Markup Language, the common language used to write documents that appear on the World Wide Web.

HTTP An abbreviation for HyperText Transport Protocol, the common protocol used to communicate between World Wide Web servers.

Link A text element or graphic within a document that has an embedded connection to another item. Web pages use links to access documents, images, sounds, and video files from the Internet, other documents on the local Web server, or other content on the Web page. Hyperlink is another name for link.

Multimedia As a general definition, multimedia is the presentation of information by multiple media formats, such as words, images, and sound. Today, it is more commonly used to refer to presentations that use a lot of computer technology.

Nesting The use of parentheses to combine several search statements into one search statement.

Paraphrasing To restate in your own words a passage written or spoken by another person.

PDF This stands for Portable Document Format. It is a file format that allows authors to distribute formatted, high-resolution documents across the Internet. A free viewer, Adobe Acrobat Reader, is required to view PDF documents.

Plagiarism To present another person's words or ideas as if they were your own.

Primary Source Firsthand evidence, based on your own or someone else's original work or direct observation.

Search Engine An online service or utility that enables users to query and search the Internet for user-defined information. They are typically free services to the user.

Secondary Source To report describe, comment or analyze the experiences of work of others. A secondary source is at least once removed from the primary source.

Server A software program used to provide, or serve, information to remote computers. Servers function in a Client-Server information exchange model. This term may also be loosely applied to the computer that is used to serve the information.

Summarizing To condense the essentials of someone else's thoughts into a few statements. A summary is shorter than a paraphrase and provides only the main point from the original source.

Truncate To use a root of a word followed by an asterisk in order to retrieve variants of the word.

Upload The process of moving or transferring a document, file, or program from one computer to another computer.

URL An abbreviation for Universal Resource Locator. It is basic sense, it is an address used by people on the Internet to locate documents. URLs have a common format that describes the protocol for information transfer, the host computer address, the path to the desired file, and the name of the file requested.

Viewer A program used to view data files within or outside a browser.

Web (WWW) This stands for World Wide Web. When loosely applied, this term refers to the Internet and all of its associated incarnations, including Gopher, FTP, HTTP, and others. More specifically, this term refers to a subset of the servers on the Internet that use HTTP to transfer hyperlinked documents in a page-like format.

Web page A single file as viewed within a Web browser. Sever Web pages linked together represent a website.

References

Chapter 1

Barstow, D., & Bergman, L. (2003, January 9). A family's fortune, a legacy of blood and tears. *The New York Times*, p. A1.

Holland, E.I.M., Ph.D. (1997). *From the Mississippi Delta: A Memoir.* New York: Simon & Schuster.

Troyka, L.Q. (2002). *Simon & Schuster Handbook for Writers* (6th ed.). Upper Saddle River, NJ: Pearson Education.

Chapter 2

The Basics of Google Search. (2002). Retrieved February 27, 2003, from http://www.google.com/help/refinesearch.html

Finding Information on the Internet: A Tutorial. (2002). Retrieved January 14, 2003, from http://www.lib.berkeley.edu/TeachingLib/Guides/Internet/Strategies.html

Gallagher, D. F. (2002, December 9). In the 'Google' economy,' businesses thrive by appearing prominently on the search engine's free listings. *The New York Times*, p. E1.

Global Warming: Fact vs. Myth. (2001). Retrieved March 3, 2003, from http://www.environmentaldefense.org/documents/382_myths.htm

Internet Searching Tools. (2002). Retrieved February 27, 2003, from http://www.sou.edu/library/searchtools

Searching FAQs. (2003). Retrieved February 26, 2003, from http://www.cln.org/searching_faqs.html

Sullivan, D. (2001, October 26). Search engine math. *Search Engine Watch*. Retrieved January 13, 2003, from http://searchenginewatch.com/facts/math.html

Cohen, L. B. (2003). Internet tutorials. *University at Albany Libraries*. Retrieved January 11, 2003, from http://library.albany.edu/internet

Whalen, J. (2002, October 30). Explaining the recent Yahoo/Google changes. *Traffick.com*. Retrieved February 26, 2003, from http://www.traffick.com/article.asp?aID=120

Chapter 3

Chokshi, M., Carter, C., Gupta, D., Martin, T., & Allen, R. (1991). Computers and the apartheid regime in South Africa. *South Africa. Guide to Internet Resources. Stanford University*. Retrieved Dec. 12, 2002, from http://www-cs-students.stanford.edu/~cale/cs201

Goldstein, N. (Ed.). (1998) *The Associated Press Stylebook and Libel Manual*. Reading, MA: Addison-Wesley.

Halberstam, D. (2002, May 20). A Pulitzer Prize-winner speaks of terrorism, life after college and choosing wisely. *USC Chronicle, 21*(29), 10-11.

Sollee, D. (2001). *Smart Marriages. The Coalition for Marriage, Family and Couples Education*. Retrieved December 12, 2002, from http://www.smartmarriages.com/divorcepredictor.html

Troyka, L.Q. (2002). *Simon & Schuster Handbook for Writers* (6th ed.). Upper Saddle River, NJ: Pearson Education.

Chapter 5

New York Times Newspaper 2001 Fact Book. (2003). Retrieved February 16, 2003, from http://www.nytco.com/company-factbook.html

Chapter 7

Evarts, E. C. (2000, July 6). Gas-guzzling SUVs muster up a makeover. *Christian Science Monitor*.